THE SECRETS OF
A HIGH-MAINTENANCE WOMAN

The Secrets of a High-Maintenance Woman

JULA JANE

JULA, INC.

Published by
JULA, Inc.

© 2005 by Jula Hijazi

For information, address JULA, Inc.,
700 Park Regency Place Suite 1402
Atlanta, GA 30326

www.thesecretsofahighmaintenancewoman.com

ISBN 0-9764588-0-2

Photographs, unless otherwise credited, are
courtesy of the personal collection of Jula Jane.

Acknowledgements

"Look Mom, no hands!"—words a mother hopes she never hears from her baby girl. Sorry, Mom, you're stuck with me. Besides, don't forget what grandmamma always says: you deserve me. Mommie Dearest, thank you for always being by my side, no matter what I do. You are the one person in this great big world I can rely on without doubt or hesitation. You are everything to me and I love you! Without you, this book and everything in it would not have been possible.

I want to say a special thank you to all the men who've been in my life. Thank you for the love, the passion, the drama, and, of course, the laughter. Most of all, thanks for the heartache—you made me that much stronger. I wish you all a life of happiness filled with whatever it is you desire.

Last, but not least, thank you to those who supported me in my quest to write my story. Your efforts have not gone unnoticed and won't be forgotten.

Photography: Kelly Blackmon
Hair: Sevin
Makeup: Olivia Johnson

Contents

Photography: Kelly Blackmon
Hair: Sevin
Makeup: Olivia Johnson

About the Author

Jula is a native of Baudette, Minnesota, a town of thirteen hundred people. A farm girl with the heart of a city dweller, she made her way to Atlanta, Georgia, by age eleven when her mother decided to pursue a career and be closer to her family. Struck by the fast life at an early age, Jula set her sights high and never looked back.

Jula knew she could never settle for an existence less than extraordinary. While her friends were outside playing, Jula was watching *Lifestyles of the Rich and Famous*, fantasizing about her great future. Never one to rely on others to make her dreams a reality, Jula began to form a business plan on life, a way to the top. She started her first job at twelve, working in the food court of a nearby mall. She walked several miles to get there, dodging traffic, with a smile on her face the whole way because she always stayed focused on the reward: money and power.

Power at the age of twelve sounds strange. Jula was missing out on class trips and such girlish activities as sticker trading and clothes swapping because her single mother couldn't afford such luxuries. Jula grew frustrated by this, so she found a job to earn enough to get what she wanted. The money gave her the power to participate with other kids.

Jula's mother remarried and had a son, but unfortunately the marriage failed before the child was born and she was forced to move into a house owned by her sister. Jula did not want to change schools, so she convinced her mom to let her get her own apartment near her current school. At the age of fifteen, entering her sophomore year in high school, Jula was living on her own, working, and attending school.

This proved quite challenging, since Jula did not have a driver's license or a car. Finding a ride became a full-time job in itself, but she did it. Finally she turned sixteen, obtained her license, and, with the help of an $800 loan from her family, bought her first car.

Living on your own as a teenager allows you to grow up a lot faster than you probably should, but Jula felt that her circumstances made her a strong woman. Jula has relied on her mind and drive, but has also been aware of her power as a woman and used it to her advantage. Realizing early on that boys/men are eager to help an attractive girl/woman with just about anything, Jula capitalized on her looks and personality and never ceases to be amazed by what men do for her, from total strangers pumping her gas to helping her pull an item from a top shelf at the grocery store. This sort of thing happens on a daily basis, yet Jula never takes advantage of people. She does, however, accept this assistance and praises them for it. They go away feeling helpful and proud, making Jula's life just a little bit easier. Jula embraces her sexuality and exudes a feminine quality that draws men in.

Jula has lived a jet-set life full of fast cars, gorgeous men, luxurious trips, and fabulous homes. She has been married and divorced twice before her thirtieth birthday, dated rock stars and CEOs, and was named one of Atlanta's most wanted bachelorettes by *Jezebel* magazine. Jula has seen the world and tasted its finest pleasures and she will teach you how to do the same.

Single again and now thirty, Jula is determined to make this decade her best. Self-employed and free to do as she pleases, Jula is living life to the fullest. She goes out almost every night while in Atlanta or spends her time traveling with one of her fabulous suitors. Through her adventures, Jula is documenting her trials and tribulations in love and lust, learning from her mistakes, and passing her newfound wisdom on to others.

She has started a column called Dear Jula, a cross between Dear Abby and *Sex and the City*, that reaches out to men and women around the

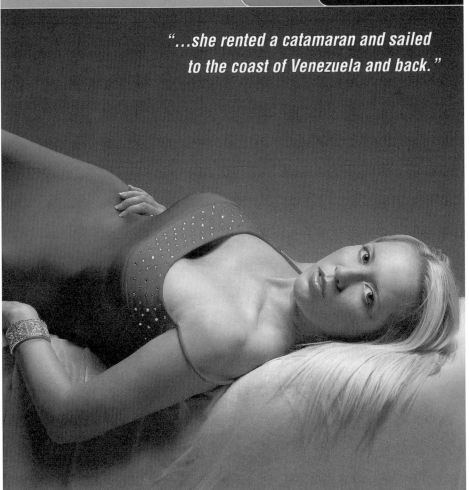

"...she rented a catamaran and sailed to the coast of Venezuela and back."

Photo by Kevin Ames   Hair by Antonio Miller, Vis-A-Vis The Salon.   Makeup by Nikole Morrow-Pettus, Van Michael Salon, Buckhead.

Age: 28 *"The most exciting thing to me is to create a new company, make it profitable, and then sell!" Jula is truly an entrepreneur; if life ever gets boring, she just starts a new business.* **Education:** Interior Design degree from The Art Institute of Atlanta; Georgia Institute of Real Estate. **Accolades:** Jula's entrepreneurial spirit in business crosses over into her personal life. She tries to live each day to the fullest with no regrets–meeting people and doing as many new things as possible. While visiting Aruba, she even rented a catamaran and sailed to the coast of Venezuela and back. Jula's drive has gotten her far. She has owned a tanning salon (which

she sold for a profit), a real estate company (which she still operates), and opened an interior design firm (which landed exclusive accounts). Jula loves her latest venture, being a Star Sales Consultant at Mercedes-Benz of Buckhead next door to Chops, one of her favorite restaurants. She also enjoys The Palm, BluePointe, and Twist. **Ideal Date:** "I love surprises, so something out of the ordinary would be great!" **Dream Guy:** "I would love a fellow entrepreneur–an exotic, handsome, successful, fun one." **The Way To Her Heart:** You'd better to love to shop, if you want to date Jula. The way to her heart is through her closet.

Courtesy of *Jezebel Magazine*

globe both single and involved, young and old. People write in, divulging their deepest secrets and recounting their most horrific dating stories, looking for advice and camaraderie. It's easier to get through life knowing other people are going through the same things you are.

Jula also has a private club called High Maintenance. It's devoted to her followers, offering advice, dating tips, social events, and how-to workshops. Most important, it brings men and women together with a single cause—surviving each other. An entrepreneur at heart, Jula has turned her hobby and lifestyle into a business.

One may wonder how Jula is able to afford this lifestyle. Most people, when they learn of her two divorces and current way of life, assume that she must have gotten generous divorce settlements. On the contrary, Jula has been in real estate since the age of nineteen and now enjoys an independent career as a result of many years of hard work. She started as a buyer's agent and then became one of the top agents in the company. After realizing a need to expand her expertise to include listings, Jula joined the most prestigious firm in town and climbed her way to the top. After three years in the business, Jula got her broker's license and opened her own firm.

With her background and education in interior design, Jula formed a company that combined her two passions, real estate and interior design. Capitalizing on her contacts, she was able to land some major builder accounts and successfully ran her own business. She had a staff of Realtors and designers along with a support staff, which allowed her to do what she does best: develop and grow the business.

When 9/11 happened, it played a major role in testing Jula's survival skills. Some of the company's biggest accounts were not paying on time or even at all since they too were faced with hard times. Jula's company went from making high six figures to almost not being able to pay the bills. After much restructuring, Jula was forced to make one of the hardest decisions of her life: close her beloved company or face possible bankruptcy. Through this whole ordeal, Jula maintained perfect credit, never paying a bill late or missing an employee's wage, even

Photography: Kelly Blackmon
Hair: Sevin
Makeup: Olivia Johnson

if she had to sell off her personal assets. She liquidated everything she could to fulfill her obligations and, after many months of struggle, was able to breathe easier, except that now her source of income was gone. She owned a house in a country club as well as an apartment in town, where she spent most of her time. The bills were coming in rapidly and, faced with no alternative, she decided to rent out her house and live full-time in her apartment. This proved to be a great move.

Exhausted from her past business obligations, Jula chose to take a break from employees and overhead and get a job. Someone bet her that she couldn't make it in the car business, so she used that as the carrot she needed to swallow her pride and work for someone else. She landed a sales position with an elite Jaguar dealer in town and within her first month was their top salesperson. She held this title for the duration of her career with them.

Six months later, Jula was earning enough money to buy a new three-story home in Buckhead and a brand new Mercedes 500SL. She also became romantically involved with her Arabian Prince. He swept her off her feet instantly, taking her to a secluded island and asking her to be his wife and live with him in the Middle East. Diehard romantic that she is, Jula accepted without hesitation. They were married in Rome, honeymooned in Positano, and journeyed to Kuwait so Jula could select her home.

Life proved to be quite daunting and very dangerous, forcing this romance to come to a premature end. Her adjustment to a new culture and completely different way of life was difficult, to say the least, but the real challenge was dealing with the constant threat from men. A woman in Kuwait, if not accompanied by a man, is at risk for being harassed and often attacked. Jula was followed everywhere she went—in stores, on the highways, and even to her home. Her husband worried that Jula, a beautiful, blond, a rarity in this part of the world, would be kidnapped and held for ransom; because he was in the oil business, his wife was a definite target.

The other challenge was Jula's desire to look her best for her husband. She dressed to please him: elegant yet sexy. He appreciated this, but feared the unwanted attention it would command. Jula toned it down, but lost a bit of herself in the process. Her husband watched his vivacious, sensual wife slowly deteriorate. The conservative ways of this world were literally sucking the life out of her and it ripped him apart to see the love of his life suffer. The woman who once sipped champagne while sauntering through a crowded room now sat desolate in a corner, longing for the life she once knew.

Jula and her husband tried to make the best of their situation, but, after much discussion, eventually decided to split up. He had no choice but to stay in Kuwait to run his father's company and, if Jula was to survive, she had to go home to pick up where she left off.

Jula moved back to Atlanta, sold her big house and most of her furniture, and bought a small condo in an elite building. She wanted a fresh start. Leaving most of her belongings scattered in the homes she shared with her husband, she now faced rebuilding yet again. She has given her real estate company a new image and ventured into the commercial market. Her client list spans the globe and she travels extensively in search of projects and investors, a perfect fit for this jet-set woman. Combining work and play is second nature for Jula, enabling her to balance a busy schedule without losing time for herself.

Jula's current passion and focus involve launching this book in a big way. Her goal is international acclaim and a position on the best-seller list within a year. True to her background of not relying on others, she has decided to publish it herself. With her understanding of marketing and how to grab an audience, Jula is going to shock and excite you with outrageous parties and national workshops, tempting merchandise, and a members-only club designed to make a high-maintenance woman out of just about anyone.

The Secrets of a High-Maintenance Woman is Jula's debut, with the sequel, *The Adventures of a High-Maintenance Woman,* and the prequel, *The Making of a High-Maintenance Woman* soon to follow. Be careful when you run into Jula. If you impress her in a good or even a bad way, you just may find yourself as a character in her latest book.

THE SECRETS OF
A HIGH–MAINTENANCE WOMAN

Introduction

DEFINITION

high (hī) adj.
a. Of great importance.
b. Eminent in rank or status.

main·te·nance (mān'tə-nəns) n.
a. The act of maintaining or the state of being maintained.
b. The work of keeping something in proper condition; upkeep.

A high-maintenance woman is a highly desirable, well put-together woman. She has a great body due to sweat equity at the gym and only "eating until she is full." Her skin is soft from twice-daily moisturizing rituals preceded by regular exfoliating treatments. She sports a healthy glow acquired from the tanning salon, leaving just a sexy g-string tan line. Her hair is colored and styled to perfection, but never too stiff for a man to run his fingers through. She has French-manicured fingernails and toenails, tasteful and very appealing. She wears just the right outfit for any occasion—a sophisticated Chanel suit for business, a Versace gown for black-tie events, and Agent Provocateur lingerie around the house. Jeans and a T-shirt to watch the game and smart slacks and a sweater to meet the parents. And for very good boys, she'll wear six-inch stiletto heels to bed.

The high-maintenance woman commands respect from those around her or quickly leaves them behind. She enjoys the finer things in life—champagne and gourmet food, the arts and culture, and, of course, jewelry. Knowing what she brings to the table, she will never settle for less than an extraordinary man, an equal.

REALIZATION

```
CLASSIFIEDS

SWM, short, fat, and bald, seeks 5'10" supermodel for
girlfriend. Must have blond hair, large breasts and a
great body. Head-turners only need reply. (404) 555-RICH
```

When one hears the term "high maintenance," one automatically has a negative reaction. Men often use it as a label for women they believe are after their money. It's funny how men use money to attract young, gorgeous women and then act indignant when these same women only want them for their money. We've all seen the older, balding, rich guy throw cash around to impress the ladies, hoping to win the most beautiful one. He later complains to his buddies that he wants to move where no one knows who he is or what he has, so that he can find someone who will want him for just him, not his money.

Newsflash, guys—quit flaunting the dough and play in your own league. If you're forty-five to fifty-five years old, balding, and, let's face it, not in the best shape, do you really *deserve* a supermodel? Perhaps you should focus on women your own age with similar qualities. What's wrong with a woman in her forties with a few wrinkles, but a nice face nonetheless, one who takes care of herself, and has a wonderful personality? Nothing's wrong with her, so why chase after the young, beauty queens? Could it be that you have a lot of money and feel entitled to have a gorgeous woman by your side? Who wouldn't? Why then would she choose you over a young, hot guy who can keep up with her in and out of bed? She just might be attracted by your

Photography: Kelly Blackmon
Hair: Sevin
Makeup: Olivia Johnson

ability to offer her a lifestyle that the hot guy can't, a life of travel and fine food, beautiful clothes and jewelry, and may be willing to overlook your appearance and focus on how much she enjoys spending time with you. You both add value to the relationship, no matter how dysfunctional it can be. If she is high maintenance, then you must be a dirty old man. Fair is fair.

Why is a rich man who dates a hot woman considered a stud, but a hot woman who seeks a rich man labeled a gold digger? We don't blame a man for wanting a beautiful woman, but we definitely criticize a woman for wanting a rich man. Let's open our minds to the big picture. If a woman takes care of herself, looking great all the time, making herself desirable to all men, shouldn't she have the right to set standards and choose accordingly?

A relationship built on beauty and money is in dangerous territory. When her looks fade, he may lose interest or, if he loses his money, she may no longer find him appealing. It's fine to have beauty and money as part of the equation, but you have a better chance at long-term survival if other things bring you together, such as similar interests and the ability to have fun with each other. If you make each other laugh, you can get through most anything.

MOTIVATION

"She's definitely high maintenance," I overhear a guy say to his buddy and realize he's referring to me. Not one to pass by such an opportunity, I strike up a friendly conversation with them, not letting on that I am aware of their opinion. We talk politics and business, a subject they can follow fairly well. I inquire about their past travels; neither of them has a passport. Impressive. I've traveled the world, but see no point in bringing that up, knowing it will only intimidate them further. They both work in software sales and have tasted a bit of success during the tech boom but are now struggling through the recession. Asked what I do, I give my usual response: real estate. We chat about property a bit, and only one of the two has ever owned a house. I just bought my seventh, but keep that fact to myself.

Wanting to impress me, they start talking about their prized possessions—their cars. One has a 5-Series BMW, the other an E-Class Mercedes. Two very nice cars, I assure them. After proving their superiority, they wanted to know what I drive. A little Mercedes convertible, I reply. Oh, the SLK? No, I say, the new SL500. It doesn't matter that I am very humble with my response; they are visibly taken down a notch. No man wants a chick to drive a better car than he does. I quickly change the subject to relationships, a fairly neutral topic, I hope. I inquire what they look for in a woman. Beauty is first on the list, with a good personality running a distant second. Each confirms that she can't make more money than he does or he will feel a bit emasculated. She also has to be available to him when he wants her; he won't compete with her career or friends. So what you're saying, I ask, is that you want a well-dressed female with a great body, gorgeous face and hair, and well-groomed, basically a woman that you can be proud to have on your arm, someone willing to put you ahead of everything else. With silly grins on their faces, they agree wholeheartedly.

I don't blame you—every man wants that, I say. I just have one question. If you don't want her to have a job that gets in the way of your time together, and she can't make more money than you, how is she going to be able to afford nice clothes, hair and nail maintenance, and a gym membership to keep looking great for you? They stare at me expressionless. "I don't know" is all they come up with. If she puts her own career aspirations aside, thereby freeing up her schedule to suit you, and allows you to pay for these items, things that you have said are important to you, would that make her high maintenance or accommodating? Would you rather have her time and pay her way, or sacrifice her time and let her work and pay her own way? Silence. I think I made my point and casually walked away.

These are typical men with average incomes and relatively simple lives and there's nothing wrong with that. They just need to play in their own league and not criticize someone because she's out of their reach. "I want a simple girl who is happy to have a beer with me and watch the game." I hear this a lot. That's great! You should have that, I tell them. It's just not going to come in the package you want it to. How often does the average guy get bored with his sweet, doting average girlfriend or wife? Every day! Deep down everyone wants that flashy red Ferrari yet ends up settling for a Toyota. Why? They are intimidated because they can't afford the Ferrari and therefore come up with reasons why the Toyota is better, even going so far as to criticize the Ferrari. This helps them justify their own inadequacies.

Anyone who takes one look at me immediately labels me high maintenance. I used to be offended by this, but since I've learned the motivation behind their statement, I can chalk it up to their own insecurities instead of my flaws. I have learned to be cordial to those men intimidated by my beauty or success, but don't date them. This frees up my time for the strong, confident man who deserves me, a high-maintenance woman who will treat him like a king.

Who Is This High-Maintenance Woman?

I am you, a woman striving to be her best in life, in love, in spirit. I am a high-maintenance woman with many faces. A man can take me to a black-tie affair, a company picnic, or put me on the back of his Harley and I will fit right in. In some ways, I am a chameleon.

I am thirty years old, blond, with ambition as well as intellect. I am a business owner, an entrepreneur through and through, and totally self-sufficient. I pay my own bills, buy my own clothes, and spend my own money.

My tastes are extravagant, making it imperative that I earn a great living to support my habit—shopping. I adore designer clothing, and my shoes cost $400–$900 per pair and my handbags in excess of $1000 each. I have a passion for one-of-a-kind pieces and refuse to be seen wearing the same dress as someone else. Vanity plays a huge role in my life. I eat whatever I want, but limit my portions to keep my figure lean and voluptuous. The word "frumpy" is not in my vocabulary. I don't own a shoe with less than a four-inch heel, and my idea of sweats are sexy Juicy Couture. My makeup is natural by day, seductive by night. Jewelry makes my eyes sparkle, and diamonds are the only stone I'll wear. Keep those cheesy sapphires away. Platinum is outstanding, but white gold is a nice alternative. The only time I'll consider yellow gold is if the right outfit demands it. Costume jewelry can be fun, but I never overdo it. I like simple elegance.

Photography: Skylar Reeves
Hair: Sevin
Makeup: Olivia Johnson

The men I date are extraordinary in their own right, possessing a trait I can't live without. They are either gorgeous (stunning, actually) or hugely successful with brains to match. I am a sucker for a fellow entrepreneur who can dance circles around me. Either way, they have to knock my socks off or they don't make the cut.

I have traveled the world, lived in the Middle East and Europe, and tasted all walks of life. I can move freely through many countries, understanding their currencies and customs with ease. I'm always looking for adventure. I will scale a cliff to get to the amazing spring below, crash a Diwaniya and hope for the best, or sail around the world with the man I adore.

My hobbies consist of reading at least a book a week, bouncing between fun novels and educational texts. I try to grow my mind every day and follow politics and current events, which also helps in conversation. Ditsy blond bimbo I'm not. I enjoy travel more than anything and usually board a plane every month, if not more. I also love to write, fiction on occasion, but my real passion is nonfiction, articles as well as books.

My palate is limited, but I will try anything once. Being a Minnesota farm girl, I crave meat and potatoes, usually filet mignon and garlic mashed. My second love is pasta, any and all. Champagne runs through my veins—I absolutely cannot live without it. Having tasted $3000 bottles of wine, I find it hard to drink the cheap stuff. I go with the flow, however, and when confronted with limited options, as is often the case in bars, I opt for a Bellini. Yummy.

I have an adventurous spirit and enjoy living on the edge. Put me behind the wheel of a powerboat and I'm a happy woman. I prefer motorized fun to jumping out of a plane. I have been known to rent a jeep and drive all over an island, exploring every nook and cranny. It's dusty and dirty and yet still so much fun. Rollerblading in the park, kayaking in the ocean, and playing a bit of touch football are high on my list. I used to live in a country club and did the golf/tennis routine but found it a bit boring (plus I'm not very good at either sport).

I like nothing better than throwing on a pair of tight jeans, a cleavage-revealing top, and my slinkiest stilettos to go hustle a pool hall. I put a little ACDC on the jukebox and let the games begin. Having won a tournament or two in my day, I can hold my own with any guy. They just don't know it up front. I am the queen at throwing a few games to lure my prey. The unsuspecting voyeur usually challenges me to a game because he wants to spend a little time with me and, before he knows it, he's lost all his cash. Sorry.

There's a side of me that is quite domestic. I can plan and cook a meal for fifty and pull it off without a hitch. Martha Stewart's got nothing on me. My table will look amazing, and the house will be perfect. I can change a filter or a lightbulb, clean and do laundry, and know my way around a fuse box. But just because I can doesn't mean I do. I also know how to hire a maintenance man and a maid.

The businesswoman in me strives for great success with whatever I may be working on at the time. I've owned several businesses, all of which I created and started on my own, wearing many hats: president, broker, designer, manager, and employee. I have a fearless quality that enables me to take risks. Some pan out, others do not, but I learn from all of them. I love to create and grow a company, but do not have the desire to work the day-to-day side of it and need an exit strategy in place, just in case.

I adore being by my man's side at a formal affair or business dinner, watching him delight in the response he gets with me on his arm. I know which fork to use, when to begin eating, how to order appropriately, and what to say or, more important, what not to say. I love to observe him in action. I'm happy to add to the conversation without dominating it, letting him shine. My personal ensemble will be appropriate for the occasion, but will nonetheless steal the show. His image will be improved by having all eyes on us. This is important to me.

I can't deny my decadence. I love to drink champagne and lie nude on the front of a yacht, flipping through *Vogue* or reading a dirty magazine. If my guy is with me, I will make love to him continually, satisfying his every need. I have such a desire to please my man, and I derive pleasure from seeing his reaction to me. The more attracted he is to me, the more motivated I am to dote on him. The man who treats me well lives the life of a king. I make sure of it.

I am open-minded and adventurous when it comes to sex, but only with my guy. Because I'm selective about who I share myself with, I am not promiscuous. I find it fascinating how the man I'm with brings out a side of me I've never seen before. The combination of his personality and mine creates a new experience for both of us. I learn something new every time I'm with a different man, yet I never crave variety. Once I'm in love with someone, that person is all I need.

Depending on his preferences, I go out of my way to keep things interesting. He may come home to find me dressed as a naughty little schoolgirl one day or wearing his favorite garters and stockings the next day. I will perform a sexy striptease if he wishes or just keep it simple and rip his clothes off when he walks through the door. I find it wildly erotic to be his and only his, with my only job in life to bring him pleasure. The thought of his coming home from work for an afternoon quickie is delightful, followed by an evening filled with hours of pleasuring each other.

I travel first class, believing the journey is as important as the destination. I like seats on a plane that recline into a bed, a flight attendant who brings me champagne with a smile instead of a frown, and a meal served on china instead of plastic. I have a driver take me everywhere I go, waiting for me between stops: Cody in L.A., Carlton in New York, and, my favorite, Charlie in Las Vegas. I'm very particular about where I stay and, when traveling with a companion other than my husband if I'm not married, I require my own bedroom and bathroom. Many of my first and second dates involve traveling together, which is a perfect way to get to know someone in a fun setting, but not the time to share a room. The two-bedroom suite is perfect, allowing me my own space, but offering a common area for us to visit.

I am pretty easygoing and if something throws a wrench into a plan, I can adapt. Suppose the hotel is overbooked and the only place available is a dive—I will go and laugh the whole time, enjoying the different experience for what it is. I am happy to hop into a dirty cab and tool around the city if that's what the day calls for and sometimes prefer a little real life to my normal luxurious lifestyle. I'll take a hole-in-the-wall mom and pop restaurant over a pretentious one most any day or a slice of pizza from a vendor on the streets of New York. Life is about enjoying the many different things the world offers and deciding what pleases you the most.

A person who meets me may find me initially reserved and distant—I take a while to warm up to people. This doesn't mean I'm not interested in getting to know them; I just take things slowly, observing more than participating. I hate when a guy I don't know hangs on me or even touches me. My body language will communicate whether you can approach me on that level. I don't hug or kiss men I'm not dating, ever.

When it comes to other women, I tend to be indifferent unless they are friends. I haven't had much luck with female friends, mostly because of jealousy. I will do anything for a friend and never judge them, but a stranger is another story. I don't like catty or bitchy women and try to avoid them at all costs. When introduced to a woman, I am friendly and make an effort at conversation, but for a woman to become my friend requires time and a sense of trust.

I have a soft spot for those less fortunate and often volunteer. I hope to have more time and money to devote to doing charity work. Rescuing enslaved camel jockeys in the Middle East who are usually three to six years old ranks at the top of this list. These poor boys are sold or kidnapped and made to live in filth with only enough food and sleep to keep them alive. The thinner they are, the faster the camel will go.

My family is very dear to me. My mom is my confidante and my sister my judge and jury. They keep me in line, always wanting the best for me and from me. If I get off track or become too much of a handful, they let me know. I will do absolutely anything for them without hesitation. I am very protective of those I love, and will make sure no harm comes to them.

Organized religion doesn't play a huge role in my life. I'm spiritual with a Christian upbringing and am curious about other beliefs. I want to study and learn about other religions before I will say for sure whether one is right or wrong. I suspect there's a little bit of truth in all of them.

I have a bit of a temper, a fiery side that comes out when provoked. I've been known to throw things and once pegged my boyfriend in the head with a biscuit. Sorry, baby. I don't believe in physical abuse and wouldn't dream of hitting someone, but I will blow off a little steam. If things get a little stale, I may even conjure up a fight to spice things up. There's an upside to this—great makeup sex.

There is a sweet side to me too. I love to crawl into my man's lap and nuzzle his neck, purring like a kitten. I want his big, strong arms wrapped around me, making me feel safe and protected. I am extremely affectionate and enjoy a man who is the same. Just don't suffocate me—we all need a little space.

The last trait I want to mention is loyalty. I am loyal to a fault. In a marriage, I will never stray or turn my attention away from my husband. As long as he is my spouse, I will be loyal to him with my body and my soul. I am also loyal to friends, never willing to sell them out for my own gain and usually do just the opposite. I give someone the world unless they cross me. Then I do the one thing I know will hurt them the most. I leave.

Addicted to love, I continue my search for Mr. Right. I am not looking for a husband or a boyfriend; I want a playmate, someone to laugh with, a travel companion, a friend, and, most of all, a sexual partner. I will not answer to anyone and don't want someone answering to me. The high I get from being "in love" consumes me, making me constantly seek a fix. It's a love/hate euphoria—you love how you feel when you're together and hate how restless and psychotic you become when you're apart. I don't need a man in my life. I take care of my high-maintenance self just fine. But I want one.

This is me. Love me or leave me as I am because I can't change. I've tried to be somebody I'm not to please other people and it just doesn't work. I lose who I am then, and it sucks the life out of me. I'm a lot of fun and a lot of work, sweet and sincere, passionate and volatile, wildly ambitious and eager to please. I have finally come to realize who I am and no longer will apologize for it. If my qualities make you think I'm "high maintenance," then so be it. I will wear that badge with honor. I am a confident, independent woman who loves her life.

Now that you know who I am and how I live, you can decide if you want to know the secrets to my success. This is a tell-all, how-to book about becoming a high-maintenance woman living an extraordinary life. You will learn how to adjust your appearance and personality to that of a high-maintenance woman, pick up dating tips from a pro, recognize when a man is lying to you, get a marriage proposal without asking for it, plus many more useful tricks of the trade.

For the men who have picked up this book, continue reading. It may be directed toward women, but you will definitely benefit from learning the secrets of a high-maintenance woman. Plus, there is a chapter dedicated just to you guys. I will teach you how to win the heart of the highly desirable, well-maintained woman of your dreams and how to keep her.

A Diva Is Born

$\mathcal{E}$very woman, no matter how beautiful, needs to reassess her image and determine if she is the best she can possibly be. Are you projecting the right look and attitude for the type of man you wish to attract? You may think so, but what if you're not? Enlist the help of an image consultant to achieve the ultimate look and style you're after. Or, if you feel you know what you want, find a great hair stylist and makeup artist and stick with them. I have been going to the same place, VanMichael Salon in Buckhead, since I was seventeen. My colorist, Sharon, knows exactly how to keep my hair just the right shade of blond and never makes a mistake. I walk in, sit in her chair, and flip through the latest magazines, knowing I'm in great hands. I never have to tell her what to do or worry that I will leave looking ridiculous.

My hair stylist, Brandon, is a dear friend. He was a member of my first wedding party and has witnessed countless relationships since. He is so talented and knows what I like but isn't afraid to try something new. I trust him completely.

Recent additions to my beauty team are Olivia and Sevin. Olivia is hands-down the best makeup artist I've ever known, and I've known several. She can make me look like anything or anyone I want, depending on my mood. One day it's Hollywood glamour and the next bombshell. Once you find a makeup artist of your own, have her teach you

A typical day in the salon

how to apply your cosmetics, but for special occasions let the pro work her magic. And what can I say about Sevin? She's cool. Brandon was detained for a photo shoot one day so Sevin filled in and the things she did with my hair were amazing. I have extremely fine hair. Thinking that it would be impossible to make it look big, I brought a few wigs and hairpieces to the shoot. She tossed them aside and went to work on transforming me into Marilyn Monroe. I've never seen my hair look so good. We did another photo shoot the next day and then she made me a rock star. Try to use a stylist who can give you the look you want for whatever the occasion demands.

It's rare for a stylist to stay in one place, so it's wise to interview them before you commit. The last thing you want is to bounce between stylists, starting over each time. Find a salon that treats you well and caters to all of your beauty needs. I like the fact my entire team works together so that I only have to go to one place. They also consult with each other if I make a change that will affect the other stylist. I'm considering getting extensions for fun and so Sevin will put them in for me and will teach Brandon and Sharon how to work on my new locks.

Every woman should treat herself to a professional photo shoot. Hire a makeup artist, a hair stylist, and a good photographer and feel like a model for a day. You will treasure these photos the rest of your life and feel just a little more confident as a result. My photographer, Skylar Reeves, is a genius. I've had many photo shoots, but no one has impressed me as she did. She knows how to set up a scene with the right lighting and angles, puts you at ease, and snaps right through, striving for that one great shot. And she gets it. It's a lot of fun being pampered and doted on all day. You definitely receive star treatment— just pick the right team. That's easier said than done. Ask people in the industry for recommendations and always call that person's references. Look through their portfolio to get a feel for their style and skill level. You may have to go through a few people before you find the one who suits your needs, but once you find her you will be thrilled.

Now that you have your team in place, it's time to transform you into a Diva. Decide what you are willing to change about yourself, what the end result should be, and let them advise you. These people are truly artists and will prove invaluable in reviving your image. And be sure to make a commitment to yourself to maintain your new look. Too often a woman gets a makeover and almost immediately slips back into her normal, frumpy routine. If putting forth a little extra effort to look fabulous is too much trouble for you, then you definitely are not a high-maintenance woman.

Your wardrobe is as important as your hair and makeup, so plan carefully. You can hire a personal shopper to help get you started, but make sure you know what you want. Spend a few days walking the malls and boutiques. We tend to stay with what we're comfortable with, but it's important to venture out of your comfort zone. Fill six dressing rooms full of clothes—even things you know you won't wear—and try them on with an open mind. You may just be surprised by what you see.

If you are a professional woman, you must balance work and play, never presenting yourself as less than an elegant, sophisticated woman. Cleavage and miniskirts do not belong in the workplace, regardless of what position you have. Secretaries and receptionists need to be just as classy as female CEOs. The way to get noticed is by having a well-polished style. A classic black suit tailored to flatter your figure with a crisp white button-down shirt, simple but striking jewelry, and just the right shoes will please anyone. Your hair and makeup should be tasteful and decade-appropriate and your fingernails manicured. People will appreciate your appearance and take you more seriously. It is a proven fact that attractive people are treated better and have a greater chance of obtaining a job or promotion over someone with a less than respectable appearance.

You have a lot more room to play when it comes to your nonwork-related image. Anything goes! First decide what type of persona you want to present. Whether a bombshell one night or a laidback casual chick the next, you always need to plan your look. I never ever want you to err on the side of trashy or silly looking. A high-maintenance woman knows how to look fabulous at all times.

Photography: Kelly Blackmon
Hair: Sevin
Makeup: Olivia Johnson

People will judge you in the first ten seconds of seeing you, so be prepared for their opinion to be based on what you're wearing and how you carry yourself. Anyone who looks at me immediately sizes me up as high maintenance. I am well dressed, perfectly manicured, and ooze confidence and they therefore assume I'm expensive. They're right, I am. Looking great takes effort and a lot of money. You must be willing to make an ongoing investment in your appearance if you want to achieve high-maintenance status. I wear top-of-the line gel nails, with refills twice a week as well as pedicures. I get my hair cut once a month and colored every three weeks. I'm a natural blond, but like the texture and body that color adds to my fine strands. The price tag for these services is $400 to $700 per month, depending on where you go. This is a basic upkeep that I will never let slide, even if it means working a little harder.

Your face is your most important asset. Too much makeup can be a huge turnoff; too little shows lack of care. If I have a big date lined up, I make an appointment with Olivia, my favorite makeup artist, to transform me into a goddess for the night. She charges $35 and is worth every penny. If your guy goes out of his way to plan a nice evening for you, shouldn't you to put forth a little extra effort for him? I think so. Looking great will boost your confidence and enable you to seduce him with ease.

Your wardrobe should represent your personality. I prefer clean-lined sleek suits and statement gowns; those by Gucci and Versace are my favorites. If a man asks which designers you like, he is probing into your personality. If I were to say Ralph Lauren and YSL instead of Gucci and Versace, he wouldn't know the real me. He would picture a more reserved conservative woman, which I'm not. If I say John Galliano and Roberto Cavalli, he will form a different opinion, one of me as more flamboyant. That doesn't mean you can't combine designers in your wardrobe. In fact, I highly recommend it. There are days when I want to throw on a fabulous Ralph Lauren sweater and riding pants and head to the country club. Other times, when I'm in South Beach, Roberto Cavalli is the only thing that will do. Just be careful when you reveal your favorites—it's a window into who you are. I use the same technique on a man. I know right away what kind of personality he has when he responds to this question. And if he answers, "What's wrong with the Jaclyn Smith collection at K-Mart?" you know he's not for you. This actually happened. I doubt he was serious, but I ran just the same.

A great pair of slinky stiletto heels will turn any man's head in your direction. Men who just wanted to get closer to my shoes have approached me from across the room on numerous occasions. There is something wildly erotic about a sexy pair of shoes that drives a man crazy. He pictures you wearing them to bed with him and can't get past that visual. Invest in at least three head-turning, to-die-for pairs of shoes with a minimum of a four-inch heel. You will quickly reap the rewards. After that, if he wants to see you in something tall and sexy, he should pick it out himself and surprise you with it.

Your collection of lingerie will also show off your personality. In the early stages of dating, he won't see what you have on underneath your clothes, but you know and will feel sexier as a result. Throw those granny panties away! A pantyline is the tackiest sight in the world. I opt for a g-string or nothing at all, making me feel a bit naughty all the time. I don't believe in wearing lingerie given to me by one man for a different man, so I let a new suitor know that if he wants to see me in something sexy, he has to pick it out himself and bring it to me. This method gets him involved and stirs his imagination.

A great wardrobe and well-maintained hair, nails, and face are essential to becoming a high-maintenance woman, but the crowning glory is your body. You have to work out and watch what you eat. I am fortunate to be able to eat whatever I want, but the key to my success is portion control. I eat until I'm full, which is usually pretty fast. I get hungry a lot and end up eating several times a day, but this is the best way to keep your metabolism going. Your complexion is affected by your diet, so remember that when you're reaching for that piece of chocolate cake. If you can afford it, I suggest you hire a dietician to get you started on a proper diet, then take what you learn and apply it. I just turned thirty and am recognizing that I can't go on eating the way

I do forever, so I'm now opting for healthier choices of food and drink. My champagne is here to stay, though.

I hired a personal trainer a few years ago, enabling me to shed twenty pounds and tone my figure. As a result, I barely work out anymore. When I do go to the gym I can exercise for a day or two and my body will bounce right back to where I want it. This may not last, but I am enjoying the benefit of my past hard work. If I decide to lose a few pounds, I quickly alter my exercise regime, jump on the elliptical trainer, and lift some weights. As I age, I know I will need to make this a part of my lifestyle rather than just a quick fix.

If you're not completely happy with your body, you may want to really devote some time and effort to changing that. Almost everyone thinks they could lose a few pounds, so grab a trainer and get to work. A solid month of working out will yield great results. We've all looked at another woman and wished we had her body, but we don't. So, work with what you have and grow to love it—you have nobody but yourself to blame for your weight and figure. Flab is not fab! A well-toned body is irresistible to a man and empowering for you. I assure you—if you do the work, you'll be amazed at the results and how people will treat you differently.

If all this sounds like too much work, by all means, ignore it and go about your day. But don't expect to draw the attention of gorgeous or hugely successful men. They put in the work, so they expect their woman to do the same. If you aspire to mediocrity, then enjoy the simple life but don't envy another woman for her beauty or lifestyle. She earned it. How does that saying go—"Don't hate me because I'm beautiful"?

A true Diva demands the best. I like to expect it, but not demand it. Nobody appreciates a spoiled princess. If the man in your life does not meet your expectations, weed him out and move on to someone who does. You never want to lower yourself by asking for things or special treatment. It should come naturally from the person who is right for you, someone who truly gets you. If you take two hours to get ready in the morning, he better be patient, realizing he enjoys the result of your

Photography: Kelly Blackmon
Hair: Sevin
Makeup: Olivia Johnson

efforts as much as you do—possibly more. I have my routine down to half an hour to an hour, depending on day or evening, but it requires organization and skill. If you are constantly running late, I suggest you reassess your regime and alter it accordingly. Being late is something we never do! Diva or not, always show other people respect, and that includes respect for their time.

There are certain daily rituals that should not be ruled out, such as skin care. I exfoliate and moisturize every morning to keep my skin fresh and healthy. When time allows, I do a deep conditioning treatment on my hands and feet as well as my hair. Do your research and try many different types of products until you find the ones that suit your skin type the best. You may consider visiting a dermatologist if you suffer from adult blemishes or want to rid yourself of a flaw. I have nothing against cosmetic surgery if it makes you feel better. Do it for yourself though, not as a result of someone else's comment. I know a man with a large bald spot on the back of his head who scheduled an appointment for hair transplant surgery due to someone's not-so-tactful remark. At the time, I was crazy about him just as he was—bald spot and all. So even though I supported his decision, I made it clear that he didn't have to do it for me. I think this made him feel great because he cancelled his appointment.

If you feel that a little Botox or a full-on facelift is called for, go for it. Just do your research and make certain you're in good hands. I've heard a lot of horror stories that will make your hair turn white, so be careful. Embrace age gracefully, no matter what it takes. Vanity rules our world, like it or not. You can look great even in your later years with a little help from a friend, "Mr. Plastic Surgeon."

My dear Diva, it's time you learned how to use your power. Know your worth and strive for everything you want, everything you deserve. Just find it in your heart to be gentle with the male species. He is helpless against your charm and beauty. Have fun!

The Seduction

Now that you look the part, let's teach you how to act it. A high-maintenance woman has a certain air about her, a touch of aloofness without arrogance, a confidence that draws attention and admiration from everyone around her. She is subtle in her approach, yet direct with her desire to please. She moves with grace, making it known that she is an elegant woman who demands to be treated with respect. All men want to be with her, but only one captures her attention at a time. She knows how to be polite and never rude.

The high-maintenance woman is intelligent and poised. She is a skilled conversationalist, endeavoring never to be called a bore. She has mastered the art of seduction and will steal the heart of anyone she chooses and do with it as she sees fit. This is a woman who knows what she wants and gets it. Why shouldn't she? After all, she has exerted the effort to become well rounded, successful, and stunning.

WEAPONS OF MASS DESTRUCTION

Eyes Your eyes are your most powerful weapon, if you learn to use them properly. You can invite a man to come talk with you simply by glancing his way, making eye contact, and slowly looking away, turning your head down, as if shy. He will appreciate the attention and seek you out.

Lips A woman's lips are irresistible to a man. A perfect pout will melt his heart and inspire him to give you whatever your heart desires. A devilish grin lets him know what's on your mind without uttering a word. And a beautiful smile—well, who can resist that?

Breasts These are our best accessories. Large or small, they complement any outfit and take it from drab to fabulous. Revealing a little cleavage will make any man putty in your hands, but be careful not to show too much skin—you want to let his imagination run wild. If you're really adventurous, you can lightly run your fingers across the top of your chest, accidentally brushing your nipple. This will drive him insane.

Hands A beautifully manicured pair of hands play an important role in seducing your prey. Use them to play with your hair and remember to keep the movement subtle, not deliberate. Gently run a finger across your bottom lip, biting the tip just a bit. The voyeur across the room will seek you out, his mind racing with fantasies of kissing you.

Legs Showing off a great pair of legs will set you apart from the crowd. Cross and later re-cross your legs, slowly letting him enjoy the show. Instinctively run your hand up and down your calf, as if you weren't aware of your actions. Let your skirt fall to the side just enough to give him a glimpse of your thigh, being careful not to expose more than you should.

Now the trick now is to learn how to put all of your assets to work at once with style and ease. Your movements must be fluid and unrehearsed so they look natural. I promise that before long this will become second nature. Men often tell me that they enjoy watching me walk through a room, saying it's as if I'm gliding, with my overall presence drawing them in. That's the key, ladies. You want to create a sense of mystery.

Photography: Skylar Reeves
Hair: Sevin
Makeup: Olivia Johnson

This may come naturally to some of you, but many will have to work to achieve it. If you want to attract the best of the best, then you must be willing to do all you can to make yourself deserving of their attention. Practice your seduction techniques at your favorite bar or restaurant and pay close attention to the reactions you get. When I first arrive at a bar or club, I hesitate for a moment at the door, letting people see me. Then I slowly wend my way through the crowd, making eye contact with anyone who interests me. If you're timid, you can pretend you're looking for someone. Once I've scanned the bar, I turn and retreat to the ladies room. I have just established my presence and, by taking it away, left them wondering. By the time I return, several men are prepared to approach me, not wanting to let another reach me first. They've had the opportunity to gather their thoughts and form a plan of action to win my attention. If you are brave and venture out on your own, the restroom retreat will always bring you comfort. It gives you a chance to regroup and decide which lucky man you will allow to get to know you.

So many components go into making a high-maintenance woman. She is well rounded, meaning she is good at many different things. What are you passionate about? Find the most exciting thing about yourself and make that part of your conversation. I lived in the Middle East for a while, so I use this as a titillating topic. Most people are intrigued and want to hear all about it. Others may be indifferent, and I then change the subject. Watch people's body language and act accordingly. Keep up with current events as much as possible. This will enable you to follow along in a conversation or begin one. And, please, know the basics—who the president and vice-president are, whether we are at war or not and with whom, and the correct pronunciation of a word, name, or place before you use it.

Have a hobby, preferably something interesting. I've taken up belly dancing as my newest craze. This is a bit unusual and therefore intriguing. You don't have to be great at everything, just good at a few things. Having hobbies and interests of your own will keep you sane when you're between dates or waiting for the phone to ring. You also need to be athletic to some degree. I don't mean being a pro golfer, but some form of proficiency in a sport would be nice, or if you prefer, a regular workout routine will suffice. Hire a trainer who will teach you how to use the equipment properly and create a personalized workout routine. We need to keep our figures trim if we are to retain our high-maintenance title.

You look great, your strut is confident, your words eloquent and interesting, and your body is toned and physically fit. Now it's time to master etiquette and domestic engineering. Knowing which fork to use and which wine to drink will boost your confidence when dealing with an elegant man. He would like to be able to include you on business dinners and black-tie affairs, but only if he knows you can handle yourself properly and not embarrass him. I studied Emily Post and every other book on etiquette I could find, both business and personal. I did this when I was a teenager and continue to do so. I haven't yet encountered a situation where I didn't know how to act perfectly. The only time I need a little assistance is in dealing with a country whose customs I'm not yet familiar with. But I assure you, I will study before I'm in that situation as I did when I moved to the Middle East. I was able to attend a royal wedding and act completely at ease. Make this a priority, and you will come out feeling invincible.

I often date older, successful men who are used to dating younger women who need help with everything from what to wear to how to eat. They tell me how much they enjoy that I know what I'm doing. This makes you stand out from the rest of the women you are competing with. My man never worries that I will be out of place or embarrass him. Make sure your man feels the same way.

I hate the term "housewife"—it sounds so plain. I prefer "domestic engineer" when referring to a woman who runs a household. Know what it takes to be a domestic goddess. Take a series of cooking classes to learn how to be an excellent cook and get familiar with stocking your kitchen for impromptu gatherings. You've heard the cliché, "the way to a man's heart is through his stomach." Well, that's true in many cases, and you need to be armed and dangerous when it comes to feeding your man. Don't do it too often, but just enough to let him know what he'd be missing without you.

Decorating your home can be challenging, so hire a professional or learn what you're doing before you label yourself an interior designer. Keep in mind that you want a man in your life, so, whether you're single or married, eliminate the floral prints and stuffed animals. No man wants to sleep in frilly sheets snuggled up to your collection of teddy bears. And, please, no pictures of mom and dad in the bedroom. Limit the clutter to a minimum, showing him that you are clean and organized. Your guy wants to feel that you will be able to set up a wonderful home environment for the two of you if he decides to make you his wife.

Now it's time to focus on the mental seduction. This is the hardest to master because you're dealing with so many different personalities and circumstances. You will have to become an expert on reading people in order to succeed at this type of seduction.

You must recognize and decide which type of seductress you inherently are and at times alter your approach, depending on your target. The following are two of the many types of seductresses.

si·ren (sī'rən) n.
1. *Greek Mythology.* One of a group of sea nymphs who by their sweet singing lured mariners to destruction on the rocks surrounding their island.
2. A woman regarded as seductive and beautiful.

The siren uses her sexual energy to lure a man in and holds him by providing an escape from his everyday responsibilities and limitations. Embody his fantasy, whether it's a Greek goddess or a preppy little schoolgirl, and he will worship you for as long as you maintain that fantasy. One of the most famous seductresses ever to live was Cleopatra. Study her methods and you will surely become a skilled siren.

Photography: Skylar Reeves
Hair: Sevin
Makeup: Olivia Johnson

co·quette (ko-kĕt') *n.*
1. A vain, trifling woman, who endeavors to attract admiration from a desire to gratify vanity; a flirt.
2. A seductive woman who uses her sex appeal to exploit men. Talk or behave amorously, without serious intentions

The coquette is calculating and always in control. She uses her sexual appeal to draw men to her and then pushes them away, causing frustration and confusion. She understands the power she has over men and uses it to her advantage while orchestrating the chase of their lives. Josephine's seduction of Napoleon is a great example of the power of a true coquette.

You must learn your man's personality and behavior to perform the ultimate seduction. He has to welcome your approach and never

Photography: Skylar Reeves
Hair: Sevin
Makeup: Olivia Johnson

know your motives, for if he detects that you are trying to seduce him, he will become resistant and skeptical. Every man is a potential victim of a seduction, with the exception of just a few. Those who don't seem to lack anything in life or are indifferent or cold toward you are almost impossible to seduce. Therefore, you should learn to recognize this and move on. What fun is a seduction when the one you're trying to seduce will never succumb to your powers?

There are dangers to a seduction. It either needs to end swiftly and suddenly, leaving you in their thoughts for an eternity, or, if you are to enter into a relationship, a second seduction is required. Remember: it is imperative that you keep the mystery surrounding you alive, for familiarity breeds complacency. Never let them take you for granted and use absence and conflict to hold their interest.

Seducing another person is exhilarating and empowering, but also tiring. More often than not, I choose not to seduce those I know would readily succumb to my methods, especially if I'm not that interested in them. I realize that I'd probably have my hands full from that point on. Be prepared for the aftereffects of your deeds—you will have men in love with you—maybe even obsessed—which is a grave responsibility. I don't believe in toying with people's emotions, so I suggest that you only target those whom you are truly interested in being involved with.

There is a surefire way out of a seduction. If you feel overwhelmed or simply no longer interested, perform an anti-seduction. This comes naturally to most women. Become clingy and needy. Call incessantly, send gifts and love letters, talk about marriage and babies. The seduced will sense your desperation, grow disinterested, and quickly move on. Your pride may stand in the way of this form of anti-seduction, so only use it when the direct approach fails. If you come right out and tell the seduced you are no longer interested, he might become that much more attracted to you and relentless in his attempt to win you back. This can be exhausting since you have moved on to another seduction. You may have to put your ego aside and drive him away with the anti-seduction. I have used this tactic, and I assure you it works like a charm.

Before you can earn a master's degree in seduction, you have to test your methods. Pay close attention to the reactions you get to every different move you make. Keep a journal documenting who, what, when, and where, noting the cause and effect of all your actions. You can test the aftereffects by periodically reappearing in the victim's life. If you made a swift and sudden exit, he will probably be quite receptive, whereas the anti-seduced will probably not take your calls or show any interest. Once someone becomes disenchanted, it is almost impossible to perform a second seduction.

Seduction is a true art form. Mold it carefully and develop your own personal style. Do as much research as you can. Read every book and article on the subject. Practice and hone your skill, and, most of all, enjoy. But be cautious because you're playing with fire.

A Class Act

Elegant, poised, sophisticated—that's a high-maintenance woman. You can be sexy and alluring while maintaining your classy image. Never mistake trashy for sexy or crass for classy; it doesn't work. You may get attention, but it won't be the kind you want. A man respects and admires an attractive woman who carries herself like a lady. A sensual woman is irresistible, while a sexually forward woman is crude.

Here are some examples to illustrate the differences.

TRASHY	SEXY
Blatant dirty talk	Suggestive commentary
Showing your boobs to a stranger	Revealing a hint of cleavage
French-kissing random guys in public	Kissing your hand and touching their face
Drinking too much	Drinking just enough
Groping those who will let you	Lightly brushing against someone
Aggressively approaching a man	Making eye contact, showing your interest
Going home with someone you just met	Agreeing to see him again another time

Photography: Kelly Blackmon
Hair: Sevin
Makeup: Olivia Johnson

CRASS	CLASSY
Asking someone to buy you a drink	Waiting for someone to offer you a drink
Running off with your free drink	Chatting for a moment with the drink bearer
Asking a man what kind of car he drives	Asking what kind of cars he likes
Leaving when hearing he drives a Toyota	Saying something nice about his choice
Asking what a man does for a living	Asking how he spends his time
Rolling your eyes when he says, "Sales"	Showing interest in his answer
Giving your digits to every guy in the bar	Giving your number to one lucky man

Let's face it, we've all done some of the things listed in the left-hand column. You are forgiven and can put that way of being behind you. It is now time for you to treat yourself as you want to be treated—like a lady. That means acting like one.

Let's touch on some of these topics, starting with blatant dirty talk. A guy will almost always turn the conversation to sex, hoping to see what you're all about. This works like a charm and we fall right into it. It's up to us to keep the conversation clean and respectful.

Example 1

Hank: "So, Sally, what do you look for in a man?"

Sally: "I like a guy with big hands and feet." He knows what she means.

Hank: (feeling that he has room to be more direct) "Would you like to see my feet?" (said with a smile)

Sally: (starts to feel offended, but continues with this line of banter) "Sure, show me."

Guess what happens next?

Example 2
Hank: "So, Sally, what do you look for in a man?"
Sally: "I like a guy with integrity and a great personality."
Hank: (hoping to impress her) "That's ironic; that's exactly what I look for in a woman. We must be made for each other."
Sally: (smiling from the attempt) "I'll be the judge of that. Tell me more about yourself."

Guess what happens next?

You are in control of the conversation from the minute a guy says hello. Keep it clean, but fun—no one likes a bore. I'll teach you the art of conversation another time. Always remember that when you talk blatantly about sex with a man you have just met, his thoughts of you will go from trying to see if you're datable to trying to see if he can sleep with you. If you're one of the many unfortunate ladies who believe dirty talk will make a guy like you, please rethink this. He will laugh and enjoy the conversation but he won't respect you.

The next example, showing your boobs to a stranger, sounds silly, but I am disappointed to say that I've seen it happen more than once. What on earth goes through a girl's mind as she pulls her top to the side, revealing her bare breast to an absolute stranger in a bar? If he wanted to see boobs, he'd be at the strip club. He's here to meet a woman he can click with and possibly date and, let me tell you, you just got ruled out of that category. Breasts are part of our power, I admit, but use them for good, not evil. Revealing a hint of cleavage makes you feel sexy while luring your prey. They will be mesmerized by what they know is there but is not readily accessible. The man will pursue you in his attempt to get closer to those beautiful breasts. If you offer him a peep show, he will have no reason to pursue you.

French-kissing in public—yuck. Nobody wants to watch another couple make out in front of them. Stealing a moment with someone you love is one thing, but kissing random guys in public is an absolute mistake as well as totally gross. The guy you're kissing may enjoy the moment, but will quickly assume that this is common behavior for you and be turned off. You have a good chance of getting him to pursue you with this tactic, but, after you sleep with him, the pursuit is over and he'll be gone. A nice way to show a man you're interested without being trashy is to softly kiss the palm side of your fingers, keeping eye contact all the while, and gently touch your fingers to his cheek. If you're really getting on well, you may touch his lips. This gets his mind going and his juices flowing yet lets him know that you are a lady and he better proceed slowly.

Drinking too much may seem fun and allow you to be the life of the party, but more likely it will make you act stupid and trashy. Slurring your words and falling all over people impresses no one. I witnessed one woman, very attractive and in her thirties, make an absolute fool out of herself while clearly intoxicated. She was talking to a bunch of different guys and asked them if "they'd rather be eating p_____" and made a slurping sound. She laughed, thinking she was hot, while they just looked at her with disgust, as did I. Not getting the reaction she was looking for, she sought out another group of guys and proceeded to come on to them with dirty talk and groping. They were turned off as well.

Drinking just enough can be sexy; it makes one less inhibited. A little mischief comes over you and you feel free to make conversation with people and enjoy your evening. I understand that it's hard to be in a bar and not have a drink—just know your limits. If you can handle two glasses of champagne and maintain your composure, enjoy. But don't ever exceed your limit.

Groping a strange man in a bar is not a good way to get someone's attention. You are sending a clear message that says, "I'm hot to trot and you're the one I want." He will either be turned off by such an aggressive move or feel lucky because he thinks he's going home with you. Think before you grope; it's trashy. Lightly brushing against someone as you walk by can be very seductive. It gets his attention, leaving him guessing as to whether you meant to do that. He will be flattered by the attention and seek you out to learn more about you.

Aggressively approaching a man is not recommended. I know many guys who say they like it when a girl approaches them, but they really don't mean it. They want to pursue you. A woman who comes on too strong will turn a guy off within seconds; she will be perceived as desperate and anything but valuable. After all, if this woman was in demand, she wouldn't have time to be hitting on guys—she'd be too busy fending them off. Human nature makes us want what everyone else does. Remember that the next time you're tempted to ask a guy, "So, do you come here often?"

Making eye contact with someone you're interested in is perfectly acceptable behavior. You're letting him know that you notice him and wouldn't mind if he came and talked to you. Men are just as afraid of rejection as anyone is and may not approach you if you don't give them a sign. Eye contact is that universal sign.

Going home with a man you just met is dangerous and perceived as trashy. You simply took the chase away from him and gave him the prize. What's left? He'll assume you do this a lot and rule you out as "girlfriend" material. I hope he was great in bed because you just got nothing out of this. Actually, let's hope you got nothing out of this (you know what I mean). If you just met a guy and he asks you to go home with him, don't get angry. Because other women's behavior has conditioned him to think that you will, simply say that you find him intriguing and wouldn't mind seeing him again, just not tonight. This will send the clear message that you don't sleep with men on the first date, which he will respect, and it will also show him that you're gracious enough not to embarrass him by acting offended by his suggestion. You will have the pleasure of being pursued by this man and eventually get to know him well enough to decide if he's worth going to bed with.

Luring my prey with a come hither stare

Before we move to the next category, I want to make one thing very clear. I am extremely liberal and open-minded about women and sex. I feel we have the right to do what pleases us and I will never condemn a friend for her choices. Carrie may not agree with Samantha on *Sex and the City*, but she doesn't judge her and is always a good friend. I am more of a Carrie than a Samantha yet I don't push my way of being on anyone else. The advice I give is for a means to an end. If you want to have as much casual sex as you can, be careful and have fun. But if it's the game you enjoy, listen and learn.

Asking someone to buy you a drink is the same as asking them to hand you a ten-dollar bill. They may do it, but they'll be annoyed and put off by your request. A man will offer you a drink if he finds you attractive and wants to talk to you—it's his choice. The best method for getting a man to buy you a drink is to not have one in your hand. I find this is considerate on your part because it leaves the door open for an easy approach: "Would you care for a drink?" Everyone wins.

Running off with your free drink is crass and should never be done. You owe the person who bought the drink the opportunity to talk with you for a moment, giving him a chance at winning you over. If the chemistry isn't happening, you can gracefully make your exit without his feeling used and your feeling guilty.

Asking a man what kind of car he drives is inappropriate and makes you look shallow. What if his response is a Toyota? Will you then turn and run? If he says a Ferrari, will you beam? You will end up looking bad, no matter what he replies. There's a way to solicit the information you want without his knowing you are doing it. If you ask what kind of cars he likes, he will light up and either talk about his prized Ferrari, happy to share the information with you without having to bring it up on his own (every guy with a nice car wants to flaunt it), or he will say that he drives a Toyota, but is working hard at saving up for a fancy sports car, talking at length about the Mercedes he aspires to.

"What do you do for a living?" Asking a man this question will make him question your motives. If you inquire about how he spends his time, he will feel as if you're interested in him, not just his bank account. Never discount his response; he may simply say "Sales," being humble or cautious and looking for your reaction. He could turn out to be the CEO of Microsoft who considers what he does a form of sales. The second way of probing allows him to tell you a bit about his hobbies, which is more important if you're looking for a playmate.

Finally, giving your digits to every guy in the bar makes you look easy and desperate. Guys notice what goes on around them and will see you doing this and think that you aren't very selective. If a man has an interest in you, he will watch you for a while before he approaches.

He's observing your behavior, especially toward other guys, to help make up his mind about whether he wants to meet you. If he sees you treat men with respect and consideration, but realizes that nobody has gotten your phone number, he'll be intrigued and want to test his ability. This will also eliminate those dreaded calls from random strangers you aren't really interested in. Instead you could have one lucky man who will be calling.

In conclusion, I want to emphasize how important it is to always be a class act. Men adore classy women and will find you refreshing. They get tired of the trashy, crass girls who, frankly, shouldn't be in public. They want a sexy, classy female whom they can be proud to show off in public. We all have a Pamela Anderson in us. Let her shine in private and flaunt your Grace Kelly side in public.

Daddy's girl

Dating 101

Women all over the world, let's band together and attain what we all want—a happily-ever-after-ending in love. This all too familiar line is somehow out of reach for most women, both single and involved. True love and happiness with a man may seem a mere fantasy, a reality that will never occur. Let's explore this notion and see if we can work to make our dream come true.

We start out as little girls idolizing our daddies. We want to be father's little Princess and win him over. We bask in the delight of his adoration of us. Hearing praise from your father as a little girl is the most wonderful thing. It is the validation from the man in our life we so desperately seek. Sadly, some little girls never feel this security; they strive for a father's affection, but always come up empty. They try to do anything they can to please him. You may think, if I graduate high school at the head of my class, he will be proud of me and love me. That didn't work. Maybe if I go to college and become a doctor like him, he'll finally love me. Nope. If I learn to play golf like him, he will surely love me. That didn't work either. Sometimes we try to live up to expectations that aren't necessarily placed on us but that we place on ourselves. A father should love his daughter whether she is first in class or last, goes on to college or becomes a homemaker, is athletic or has two left feet. Our daddy should be the first to offer us unconditional love. Here is where so many of our lifelong problems with men begin—with the father-daughter relationship.

I am sad to say that very few women have ever experienced unconditional love from a male figure. Consequently, they are always setting goals to achieve in hopes of deserving a man's affection. Wouldn't it be wonderful to hear "I love you, baby girl, no matter what." How powerful this statement would be in a woman's life to know that she is worthy of love simply for who she is.

The little girl grows up and now seeks love and approval from a potential mate, partly to fill the void left by her father and partly to satisfy our culture's image of not being complete without a man in our life. We meet that man who makes our stomach flip and our heart flutter, and then we proceed to sabotage our potential for happiness. We've all done it. The question is why, followed by how can we learn to do the right thing?

I have explored the dating habits and thoughts of men and women around the globe in hopes of finding some answers to this perplexing phenomenon. My eyes have finally been opened by several personal experiences and I want to show you the reality of how men are and how they want us to be. I am the queen of doing the wrong thing when it comes to men, but am working hard at changing my ways. Let's learn and grow together and enjoy our newfound power over the opposite sex.

GAME ON

Let's face it, we girls know what we want from a man and we know what a man wants from us. The trick is getting what we want while letting him think he's in control and getting what he wants. Ultimately, a woman seeks security and love from a man usually translated into marriage. A man wants sex. Simple.

Typical Scenario: Man meets woman. Man buys woman drink. Says nice things to her. She tries on his last name. Thinks it's perfect. Man buys woman another drink. Thinks he's gonna score! Man tells woman she's the prettiest woman in bar. She believes him and beams. Man asks woman to go to his place to give him decorating ideas. She thinks he wants her to move in so she should definitely give him decorating advice to suit her taste in her new home. Man takes woman to his place, lights candles, and gives her a glass of wine. She thinks he's so romantic. He thinks he's smooth and is gonna score. Man gives woman the tour of his bachelor pad, saying it just needs a woman's touch. She hears, "I want to marry you"; he's thinking "I'm gonna score!" Man shows woman his bedroom and kisses her. She melts. He scores. Man takes woman back to her car and says, "I'll call you tomorrow." Woman goes home and plans the wedding. Man never calls woman. Woman wonders why.

Hello, ladies! Are we nuts? Why should he call? A man likes to hunt, to chase. He wants to feel as if something is out of his reach. If given a chance, he will pursue you.

THE THRILL OF THE HUNT

Picture a man who goes deer hunting. He has on his camouflage attire, carries his favorite gun, and formulates his plan of action. He ventures into the woods in search of that ten-point buck. The thrill of the hunt excites him, gets his blood flowing. He steps five feet into the forest and is confronted by a deer holding up a sign with a bulls-eye on it. The man shoots his prey, throws it in the back of his truck, and goes home feeling disappointed. That deer threw himself at the hunter much like we throw ourselves at any man who pays us attention. Boring. Had the deer valued itself more, it would have turned and run, waiting for the best man to win it in the hunt of a lifetime. There are many hunters out there willing to pursue you. Run and don't look back. When the best man captures your heart, you both win.

"I shouldn't have to play games. If a man truly loves me it will come naturally." If that's your philosophy on dating, let me ask you one question: How's that working for you? I'm not a fan of game playing either, but I do believe in male-female roles and setting the stage for romance to unfold. If we set our standards and don't waver from them, a man who is genuinely interested will live up to those standards for fear of losing us if he doesn't. Men, much like children, want boundaries.

CHIVALRY LIVES!

I want the man in my life to treat me like a lady, which includes opening my car door. If he forgets, I quietly let him remember simply by remaining in the car or standing in front of the door, but not opening it. He gets the hint and appreciates that I did not bring attention to his error. Chivalry is not dead if we don't kill it. I have to give a few men a break due to the fact that we women have confused them. Some of us act offended when a man opens a door for them. I find this sad. Are we that sensitive that we mistake a man's grace for an insult?

My second husband won me over with his genuine chivalry. He always opened my door without fail, stood when I got up from the table, discreetly paid the tab, and always walked beside me, making certain he was closest to the road to protect me. All of this from a twenty-seven-year-old gorgeous, rich, intelligent, sophisticated man. Ladies, these men do exist and you deserve them. Hold out for your Prince Charming, no matter how many frogs you have to kiss.

HOT PURSUIT

Many women pursue men instead of letting them pursue us, often believing we shouldn't have to wait for a man to call or ask us out in this day and age. I believe this is an excuse for those of us not patient enough to wait. Go ahead and invite the guy you like to dinner and go one step further and pay for the meal. You've just accomplished nothing. He may accept, but I guarantee he will not pursue you. Picture the deer inviting the hunter out to the woods and the deer chasing the hunter. What is he going to do? RUN—that's what.

The phone game has to be one of the most nerve-racking situations in the world for singles. When is it too soon to call or too late? Should I call him or wait for him to call me? Let's break this down and make it simple. Do not under any circumstance call him first! If you meet a man and he asks for your number, give it to him (only if you want him to have it) and wait for his call. I don't care if a month goes by—do not Google him or call. It won't work. A guy struggles with a similar dilemma, but one opposite from ours. He has to decide when to call without looking too desperate or nonchalant. If he calls immediately, we think he's too into us. But if he waits too long, we're upset and don't think he's interested. I can hear you now, "I don't want to play games; he should just call when he wants to." I wish it were that simple, but I guarantee that you will react the way I described whether you know it or not. It's human nature.

Once the calls have begun, we must follow the same simple rule: do not under any circumstance call him first. I can't stress this enough. When we call a man, we are pursuing him—the duck using the duck call instead of the hunter. It just doesn't make sense. You may hear guys say they like it when a woman calls them. They are lying or are delusional; they don't like it. You may and should return a call within a reasonable amount of time. Here is where real game playing can begin. I call it Power Ball. Once he has left you a message, he has tossed you the Power Ball. You now have the option of calling him back or not, knowing that his ego hangs in the balance. If you ring him immediately, you seem desperate or too into him. If you wait a day or two, he may become intrigued, if not a little smitten with you. Wait too long and he will get mad because you hurt his pride but he'll still be interested.

This is not an exact science and should be altered for each individual situation, but it can be used as a general guideline. Keep in mind that the minute you return his call you are tossing the Power Ball back to him and must now wait for him to respond. Monitor your emotions and thoughts while you wait for him to call you back and you'll get a glimpse into what he is feeling when the role is reversed. Empowering, isn't it? Two days have passed and you haven't heard from him. Your mind begins to wander. Maybe he lost his cell phone and didn't get my call so I should call him at home. NO! He got your call; he just hasn't returned it yet, by choice. You can come up with every excuse in the book yet the answer is always the same. Be patient. He'll call.

CAN'T BUY ME LOVE

I will say this once, girls. Do not, I repeat, do not buy a man presents. This will convey that you are not worthy of his affection on your own accord, therefore you are trying to buy him. I cannot tell you how many men have told me stories of women showering them with cute cards, flowers, and presents. Their response is to get turned off and run. The only time when gift giving is appropriate is on his birthday and Christmas, but only if you are in an exclusive relationship. Making inexpensive gifts for him is not allowed either. Compiling the greatest love songs of our time onto a special CD will result in gagging followed by running. Also, do not give him nude photos of you via Email or messenger. It's not sexy—it's weird. For that matter, don't give him pictures at all, with or without clothes. If he wants a picture of you, he'll request it. Ask yourself why you want to do this. If it's because *you* like receiving gifts, and therefore your man will enjoy it as well, guess again. He won't. Recall the *Sex and the City* episode when Charlotte bought her new man expensive briefs. He flipped and left her. It happens all the time.

MAID OR MISTRESS

Okay, ladies, let's dig deep and find our self-worth as we discover ourselves becoming our man's maid. Put down the laundry, step away from the dishes, and act like the Goddess you are. He doesn't want his woman doing his dirty work around the house. On the contrary he wants you to command respect and let him take care of you. He can hire someone to clean the house, but he can't hire someone to be his girl. I know you want to show him how potentially great a wife you'll be but, face it, he wants a sex goddess around the house, not a maid. The best thing one man said to me was that the only thing his woman should make for dinner is reservations. That is a man to be loved! Don't get me wrong; cooking a romantic dinner for you and your man can be quite delicious—just don't let it become a daily routine of expectation and boredom. This same man was adamant about not letting me get my hands dirty around the house.

HONEY, I'M HOME

You have a home, so don't take his. When we begin an intimate relationship with a man, we often visit each other's homes, sleeping over and playing house. We start to leave personal belongings at his house for "convenience"—a toothbrush, maybe some feminine products, extra panties, our favorite CD. Two things happen here: he begins to feel suffocated, and you begin to feel attached. I recommend that you put together an overnight bag with your essential items, taking it to and from his place but never leaving it there. By doing this, you are respecting his space and liberating yourself. You are showing him that you aren't completely whipped and have a life outside of him. For all he knows, this overnight bag may travel to other places besides just his home. I know this sounds silly, but, believe me, it works. Before long, he will yearn to have you all to himself and move toward a stronger commitment.

This goes both ways. Do not allow him to leave his things at your place. This will make him wonder why, plus it will leave him feeling a little shunned. This is good for a man. If you encourage him to set up house in your place, he'll feel suffocated again and back away. The other reason for these tactics is to create a sense of inconvenience. If he has to put forth effort every time he wants to see you, he will instinctively move toward a commitment quicker to make his life easier.

I LOVE YOU

Such a sweet sentiment can be the curse of death. Never tell a man you love him first. Let him be in control of this statement. Every man I've ever been with has always been the first to say, "I love you," making him feel like he's chasing me, trying to make me love him back. More than half of the times I've been told this, I didn't repeat it back. I wasn't playing a game, I simply didn't feel it yet. I won't say it just to make a guy feel good. The best response when you're not ready to say it back is, "I love the way that sounds. Say it again." You're sparing his feelings at a very vulnerable moment and setting the stage for the time when and if you do share those same feelings.

How many of you have told a man you love him within a few days of dating? You know who you are. Why did you do that and what reaction did you receive? Every time a man has done that to me, I go running in the opposite direction. I know there is no way that he can be in love with me so soon, so I take it as a line or sign of desperation. Keep those words in a safe and give the combination to your best friend with instructions not to let you into that safe without a signed Act of Congress.

KISS ME, YOU FOOL

Never kiss on the first date! I don't care if he is the hottest guy you've ever laid eyes on and you're overcome with lust, it is a bad idea. Leave him guessing whether you find him attractive. I used to wait until at least five dates to let a man kiss me. Several suitors would ask why I hadn't kissed them, making for an awkward moment but keeping them in suspense. I wish I could say this was calculated, but, honestly, I wasn't comfortable letting someone I barely knew touch me. The real truth is that I was afraid of his being a bad kisser and my having to endure it.

Kissing is very intimate, in my opinion, so I prefer to hold off until I have chemistry with someone so I can enjoy it all the more. I date a lot and choose to keep any physical contact to a minimum until I decide if I'm going to keep them around for awhile. Never be afraid that he will get mad and not date you anymore. He won't. A good chase can't be tossed aside—his ego won't allow it.

And never kiss in public, especially at a bar. This makes you look cheap in his eyes and everyone else's. It's not seductive but a bit slutty. Many free-spirited sexually charged women are out there who feel they should be able to express their sexuality and not hide it. I agree to a point. If your goal is to have as many one-night stands as you can, then be my guest and kiss away. But if you want to enjoy the feeling of being pursued, keep those lips to yourself.

AVAILABILITY CONFLICT

What has more value—an object that is hard to acquire or one readily available? Collector's items achieve that label for one reason: they are hard to get. We pay more for Gucci than we do for BCBG. Why? The sense of limited availability along with the status that the item represents are definite factors. If every time your guy calls and you answer, he will perceive you as being very available to him. If at times you don't take his call—sometimes for days—he will stay on his toes, feeling a little anxious. Mr. Big on *Sex and the City* was dating a famous actress who would never take his calls but would call him often enough to keep his interest. He was going insane, saying to Carrie, "She can reach me, but I can never get her." This method works like a charm. Practice the same method when it comes to dates. You can't be available every time he asks you out. Set basic guidelines and stick with them. A date for a Friday or Saturday night should be set at least three days before; weekday lunches or dinners carry a two-day rule. Never accept a date for the same day. If he doesn't value you enough to plan ahead, he isn't worth your time. I love spontaneity and encourage you to enjoy offers such as trips and exotic adventures with limited notice. Just make sure you aren't an afterthought or replacement for someone else. There is an exception to this rule—the hugely successful man who travels a lot for work. You need to be flexible with your time if you want to date this type of man; just don't let him take advantage of the situation.

Don't blow off plans with your girlfriends to accommodate a man. This will show him that he takes precedence over everyone, empowering him a little too much. I can assure you that he won't put you ahead of his pals. In fact, I've been dating a CEO of a huge company recently who had to have drinks with his guy friends before we could go to dinner. This happened on our fourth and fifth dates. He used the guise of business as an excuse, but I quickly found out otherwise. It's yet to be determined if he'll get a sixth date.

Just to keep him guessing, turn him down every so often without giving a reason. Simply thank him for the invitation, let him know you can't make it, and suggest perhaps another time. Women tend to give too many details, not allowing a man's imagination to run wild. Let him wonder who's taking precedence. It'll drive him mad. Don't fall victim to endless questioning. Who were you with, where did you go? It's none of his business unless you're his wife.

WHY BUY THE COW WHEN YOU CAN GET THE MILK FOR FREE

You'll soon learn I'm not a big fan of girlfriend rules. I think the term "girlfriend" gives men control over us without our realizing it. We become completely devoted to a man, forsaking all other potential

Look out world—I'm just getting started

suitors—basically pretending to be his wife. He now has you completely to himself, so why would marriage enter his mind? It probably won't. It is statistically proven that couples are less likely to get married when they live together first. I live my life two ways: single or married.

As a single and fabulous woman, I feel entitled to date whomever I choose and do whatever I want without answering to anyone. Unless I am sporting my man's last name, I'm free to "try on," a term I've grown to love, as many different men as I see fit. If someone steals my heart and becomes my husband, I will never turn my attention from him. I am loyal and devoted, which I feel you should be in marriage— but only in marriage. The idea of an exclusive relationship without marriage is absurd. You have your house, I'll have mine, and we'll agree to not see anyone else. We'll spend every night at each other's house with the exception of "guy's and girl's night out." We'll take years to decide if the other is good enough for us and eventually break up or cheat on each other. I believe that you know right away if you want to marry someone. If not, enjoy—but don't commit or, worse, pretend to. Remember: this is spoken from a woman twice divorced.

Men Lie, Women Gossip

Have you ever heard the joke, "How can you tell if a man's lying?" The answer: "His lips are moving." I fear there's some truth to this. Here is one woman's story of betrayal.

A married man—we'll call him Richard, Dick for short—kisses his wife goodbye and heads for the airport on a "business" trip. Dick lands in Atlanta and proceeds to his favorite bar to meet his buddies for "a guy's weekend," as they like to call it. They drink beer and hit on as many waitresses and single unsuspecting women as they can. Armed with a good buzz and enough phone numbers to last a lifetime, they then make their way to the nearest strip club, with Dick calling his wife on the ride over to let her know he arrived safely and is turning in for a good night's sleep. She is happy to hear his voice and feels relaxed, knowing he is safe and sound. I love you, they coo, and hang up. She goes back to running after the kids and he saunters into the strip club for a little mischief.

(To the guys reading this and calling me bitter, let me ask you this: how would you feel if you really were on a business trip and, after you called your wife, she hung up the phone, having just reassured you that everything was great and she loves you, only to roll over and continue having sex with the neighbor? Let me go out on a limb here and say you probably wouldn't like it—you might even be crushed.)

Photography: Skylar Reeves
Hair: Sevin
Makeup: Olivia Johnson

Back to my story. Dick and his friends grab a table closest to the stage and blow wads of cash on strippers, paying them to dance naked for them and make them feel like big shots. Hours pass and after striking out with the dancers, they decide to switch it up and visit a nightclub. Jackpot! Dick hits on a young, blond hottie eager to please. He flirts with her, using all his best lines, and finally convinces her to go back to his hotel. He doesn't have a car and his friends want to stay at the club, so she drives. Bambie turns out to be quite a minx in the sack and Dick goes to sleep thinking he's still got it. The next morning, realizing that Bambie has already left, he goes back to sleep for a couple hours. Unbeknownst to him, his wife called his cell phone to wish him a good morning and tell him she misses him, only to hear the voice of a strange woman on the other end. Dick left his phone in Bambie's car and she answered it. Bambie tells his wife that he forgot his cell phone in her car. Not able to reach Dick, his wife calls one of his buddies, recounting what just happened. He plays dumb and says he'll find Dick and have him call her right away. Horrified, Dick hears the news and, with his buddies' help, concocts a lie to tell his wife in hopes of getting out of the doghouse. Because he had told his wife he went straight to the hotel and to bed, his options were limited. He finally decides to say that he couldn't fall asleep and went down to the lounge for a drink. He brought his cell phone with him in case she called and must have left it in the bar. The only thing he can think of is that some woman must have stolen it and said he left it in her car so she wouldn't get busted for stealing. Lame!

This foolish woman believed him. She must really want to stay in a dysfunctional marriage or she wouldn't put up with such things. Ladies, we know when we're being lied to and often choose to ignore it, not wanting the relationship to end. If you let it slide once, you give him a license to lie, cheat, and steal from you. I've had two marriages, neither one involving infidelity, so I guess I can't say for certain what I would do, but I would hope I'd have enough self-respect to get out.

It breaks my heart for all the women I've never known or met whose husbands are cheating on them. Many of my first husband's employees and associates were cheating on their wives, openly bragging about their affairs. It made my stomach turn, but I had to keep my mouth shut. The hardest part was on the rare occasion I ended up at dinner with one of these guys and their wife. I'd observe the wife seemingly happy with her husband, talking about their children. Did she know about his affairs and, if she did, why hasn't she left him? Should I mind my own business or is it my responsibility to tell her what I know? I struggled with this decision, always opting not to interfere. To this day I feel guilty, wondering if I did the right thing. If my husband were cheating on me, I'd want to know—no matter what. That way I could leave him and one day find someone who deserves me. So many women chose to stay, ignoring the obvious signs, pretending everything is okay. I suppose they prefer the security of the marriage to their dignity and the idea of supporting themselves.

Being lied to is the worst offense a man can commit. It makes me feel as if I'm insane. Men lie about more than just cheating; they often lie about who they are or what they have, hoping to win you over by impressing you. I have studied psychology and behavior, not to mention body language, and almost always know when I'm being lied to. I didn't always have this skill and suffered much heartache as a result. Determined not to be misled or made a fool of ever again, I have become a personal lie detector. Men have told me on numerous occasions that I'm too intelligent and can see right through them. This ruins their image of themselves after they've presented their lives a certain way, only to be discovered. I'll share a few personal stories with you.

Story 1: I met a guy in a pub; we'll call him Dick. (I seem to like this name for these stories.) He was gorgeous and charming. He volunteered a lot of information about himself without my even asking. I told him how much I love to travel and he agreed, telling me he too was a travel buff and owned property in Hawaii and the French Riviera. He said he'd love to take me there someday. This is a good sign, I think, determined to find a playmate who enjoys the same things I do. We chat a bit more, discussing real estate, my profession and passion.

Dick then tells me about the house he just bought. He said he sold his house in St. Ives Country Club and bought a new one in Dunwoody, but he's in an apartment right now because of an erosion problem. He said the house was practically sliding down the hill and consequently was suing the builder. I told him I knew most of the builders in town and would be happy to help him. He thanked me, but declined and said that his aunt in New York, a big-time attorney, was handling his case. I found this story a bit odd, but let it go. We were together a lot in the following weeks, exchanging personal stories and interests. He was a dream come true—absolutely stunning, with a great career, someone who loves to travel, and has owned property, clearly sharing my passions. I was falling fast and so was he. He planned a wonderful birthday party for me at the pub where we first met and told me he loves me. I was shocked and didn't say it back, but I felt it.

Now head over heels in love, I was past the point of no return. As we spent more and more time with his friends, I began to hear and see discrepancies in what he told me about himself and what they said about him. In a nutshell, he had never owned a home in the United States much less the French Riviera. He doesn't travel much at all, except for business, and has never been out of the country. I thought it strange that in the two months we had been together we hadn't gone anywhere together and his lawsuit wasn't progressing. Plus he never wanted to show me his house. In the beginning of a relationship, I like to give a guy space and not ask too many questions. This is a time to enjoy each other, not play twenty questions. Sadly, I'm finding that this may not be the best idea because I keep falling for the wrong guys based on the lines they feed me. Everything I knew about the man I was in love with was a lie.

The part that upsets me is that I wasn't able to chose to spend my time with him based on who he is but instead on who he portrayed himself to be. As long as I believed in him, his lies were a reality in his mind. I truly think he thought a lot of the stories he told were true. I faced a dilemma. I was in love with the person I thought he was, someone with similar interests and goals as my own, an ambitious, financially successful, worldly man, but am I in love with the man he truly is? It would be easy to say yes and stay with him, but the answer is no, I'm not. How can I love a man I don't respect? With tears in my eyes and a broken heart, I eventually left him. Would I have dated him in the beginning if I had known the truth about him? Probably. He possessed enough of the qualities that I look for to make up for the ones he was lacking. But it was too late. The one trait I can't abide is lying.

Story 2: This one is short and sweet, kind of cute, but a clear sign of what was to come. I began to date a man in my building who told me he was forty-one. I was twenty-nine at the time and had had success with dating older men, so I thought nothing of his age. We were on our way back from New York when I asked to see his passport. He held it out for security and I was curious to learn where he's been, but he refused. I persisted, not understanding what the big deal was. He told me he would explain another time, but not now. I pressed, yet he never conceded. He also wouldn't let me see his driver's license. I couldn't understand what he was hiding. I had a friend do a legal background check on him, revealing not only his age but also his real name, not the one he gave me. He was actually forty-five and his last name was the same but the first completely different. I didn't say anything right away until one night in bed when I asked him if he didn't want me to see his passport because of his name and age. He reluctantly agreed, admitting he thought I wouldn't date him if I knew his real age. Lying about his age was a bit endearing and I let it go. Unfortunately, this was a red flag that I overlooked. In the end, he proved to be a liar on many levels. I found out that he had a girlfriend in the same building; he told me they had broken up. To cover this big lie, he told many small ones. Realizing the kind of man he was, I left him.

Story 3: I was on a first date with a handsome guy, anxious to get to know him. We had a lot in common and seemed to enjoy each other's company. As I usually do in the beginning, I told him that I'm seeing a few people and until I settle on just one man I'm not sleeping with any of them. I like to be completely up front, giving the person the chance to decide if he wants to continue dating or move on. He responds by telling me that he definitely wants to keep seeing me and respects my method of dating. He then tells me that he's doing the same thing—in the last seven years he's only been with five women, three in long-term relationships and two that were short-lived flings. Having recently broken up with his girlfriend, he hasn't slept with anyone since. He admits that he's dating a couple people, but definitely not sleeping with any of them.

I don't believe a word out of his mouth and tell him as much. He insists he's telling me the truth and, since it doesn't really matter at this stage in the game, I let it go. A few dates later he tells me how similar we are, calling me the female version of him, a line I've heard so many times. Knowing I'm not ready for an exclusive relationship, he suggests we agree to have sex with only each other, but continue to date other people. How nice. I don't think so. That never works—jealousy always creeps up on one, if not both parties. Still not committed but growing emotionally involved, I discover the truth about him. One of the girls he's dating approaches me, angry that he's with me. She tells me that they've been sleeping together for months and she's tired of catching him cheating on her. Evidently, she was under the assumption that she was his girlfriend as well as the only person he was sleeping with. I was just glad to find out what he was like and leave him before I got too involved. There is something to be said for taking things slowly—it allows you time to see if they are worthy of you.

I don't have a problem with a guy I'm casually dating seeing other women. I just want him to be as honest with me as I am with him. I give him the truth and let him decide what to do with it. Why is it that so many men tell us what they think we want to hear instead of being truthful? Could it be that they're afraid we won't date them if we know the truth? That's a risk they should be confident enough to take. I am, and because of it I don't have to lie.

These are hard times we live in. Tainted by the lies we've been told, how can we ever let our guard down and trust? I don't know that we can. Just when you get comfortable and think you have Mr. Right, he reveals himself as Mr. Wrong. I struggle with the idea that I will never be able to believe what a man tells me again, or to fully trust him. I sound cynical, I know, but the problem is that every man I've ever known has lied to me.

Have you ever found yourself pondering if this is a lie you can live with or one that will make you leave? You fear you will never meet a man who won't lie to you, so maybe you should stay with the liar you know. I've been there, but once we all start holding men accountable, they will have no choice but to straighten up. There are some countries that cut your hand off for stealing; we may not be able to cut their lips off for lying, but we can definitely sever their connection to us. If they knew without a doubt that we would leave them if they lied, I bet they'd think twice before opening their mouths.

I'm not trying to male bash—I love men, I just want to open your eyes to reality and help you make an informed decision about how to proceed when faced with a lie. Don't ever lose sight of the fact you are worthy of the truth, the whole truth, and nothing but the truth so help them God for Hell hath no fury like a woman scorned. If your gut tells you he's lying, he probably is. Don't ignore the signs. I've learned over the years how to determine when a man is lying about being married or having a girlfriend; my most recent relationship ended when I found out the man I was dating did in fact have a girlfriend. We'll be consistent and call him Richard. We went on a business trip together that turned romantic, each of us confiding to the other our current dating status. I let him know I was recently divorced, just days actually, and he said he had just ended a five-month relationship with a woman he was no longer interested in. He told me that they had been dating since February and around the fourth of July she flew back to Chicago, where she's from, to break up with her boyfriend so she could be free to date him. He realized while she was gone that he no longer felt the same way about her and gradually ended the relationship. He let me know that she was very emotionally needy and dependent, so he hasn't cut her out of his life completely but hopes to very soon. He can't stand it when women cry, so he keeps putting it off. He also told me about an old friend of his whom he has no romantic interest in, even though she's in love with him. He told her that they will never be more than friends, yet he knows that she thinks one day they'll "head off into the sunset together." He assured me that I have nothing to worry about from her and that he doesn't want to end their friendship because she was there for him when he fell ill with a heart condition and he feels obligated to her.

I made it very clear that I don't date married men or men with girlfriends. He reassured me that he is definitely eligible. I had no reason to think he was lying, so I believed him and agreed to casually date him, making it clear that I plan to see other people as well, at least for now. Things progressed rapidly—our chemistry was mind-blowing. We live in the same high-rise and consequently we agreed to keep our relationship private, away from the staff, which meant we did not leave the building together. I don't remember who initiated this idea, but I know I was happy with the arrangement.

Our first few dinner dates in Atlanta consisted of our meeting at a restaurant, either Chops or Bluepointe, his two favorites, or in the parking lot of the Ritz and then riding together. Consumed with wanting to keep my affairs private, I thought nothing of it until we went on our first trip. I offered to have my driver pick us up at the building, but he opted to meet me at the airport, saying he had a lot of business to tend to that day and would already be near the airport by the time we were leaving. I thought this was odd, but let it ride, wondering if he was trying to hide me from his ex-girlfriend. He had told me that she was not beautiful and would be devastated if she saw him with me and asked me to be compassionate, so I complied.

We spent a week in L.A. and several nights in Las Vegas having the time of our lives. He kept asking me if I was falling in love. I was literally weeks out of my divorce and did not want a relationship, so I did everything I could to keep it light, always dodging those questions. By the end of the trip, I was definitely falling for him. It was probably the most romantic time I've spent with someone and, being a hopeless romantic, I couldn't avoid his spell.

When we returned to Atlanta, I rode home with him, but we agreed to park and handle our luggage ourselves rather than letting the valet tend to us. I guess we both still were not ready to come out of the closet. He kissed me in the elevator and asked where we went from here. I told him it's business in Atlanta and dating when we're away. I don't know why, but I just kept pushing him away. Actually, I do know why. I didn't want to cut off communication with my ex-husband and I still needed to play the field a bit. I just wasn't ready to be in a relationship. When we were in Las Vegas, he asked if I wanted to stay through Labor Day, but I declined. I was feeling a bit suffocated and actually needed to get back to work. He let me know that he was considering bringing his sons back out and would be gone for a few days. I encouraged this, wanting him to spend some quality time with his boys. Here's where the story gets interesting. I used my credit card to initially book the hotel for us, then Richard had them put all the charges on his card when we checked out. I was looking at my credit card statement a day or two after we returned and saw that those charges were still on my card as well as a charge for a future reservation. I called the hotel to inquire about the new charge and was told that it covered my reservation on September 2–4, that coming weekend. I let them know that I didn't make a reservation and asked how to cancel it. The clerk told me what to do but also warned me that the hotel was overbooked and, once I cancelled, I wouldn't be able to reschedule. I realized that Richard may have booked a room for him and his boys, so I decided to check with him first.

He was clearly surprised by this information, saying, "Why would I book a trip for just two nights to a place a four-hour plane ride away?" He said that he took the liberty of booking a room for us in October in case we decided to come back and that they must have gotten the dates wrong. I let him know I was going to cancel the reservation, but he said for me not to bother. He would do it because he wanted to make sure the other charges were taken off my account. Two days later he was gone, heading somewhere for the weekend with his sons. I didn't ask where they were going and he didn't offer any information. Just before he left, he brought me a stunning necklace from Tiffany, took me to dinner, made love to me, and asked that we talk every day while he is away. I knew I'd miss him, but needed the time alone to get some work done. He consumed so much of my thoughts and energy that I had not been able to focus on much else. The day after he left I checked my account just to make sure everything was taken care of and saw the reservation charge again. I called the hotel and asked why they hadn't removed the charge since we had cancelled the reservation. The clerk explained that it was still there because I checked in last night. My heart dropped. I knew without a doubt that I had been lied to. I did a little investigating and discovered that Richard had in fact checked in to a similar suite that we had shared just days before. I didn't know if he was there with his boys, but I felt the sting of another woman. The only reason I could think of for his dishonesty was if some other woman was involved. It puzzled me because I thought I had made it clear that we were free to date other people and therefore he did not need to lie.

Days went by and I didn't hear from him. I left one message but never heard back. He finally called, saying he'd be back in Atlanta in a couple days and asked if he could visit me the night he arrived, even though it would be late. I agreed, more out of curiosity than desire. He told me his boys weren't able to travel with him, so he had been visiting potential investors in L.A., Vegas, and Chicago. I knew for a fact that he had been at the Bellagio every day for the past week. He was lying, again. But why? He got back when he said, but didn't call me until the following night. He asked if I could fit him into my schedule for breakfast the next morning. I agreed and met him at the Ritz Carlton with every intention of having this be the last time I'd see him. I had a few Mimosas before he arrived and was ready to probe him for information. I was able to find out that he had been at the Bellagio the whole time and had taken his ex-girlfriend with him. He said he did it out of guilt and as a way of saying goodbye to her for good, assuring me that he would no longer be seeing her. Here is where I went wrong—I believed him. Actually, I didn't really believe him, but I rationalized that he was within his rights to see other people. The only thing he did wrong was to lie, which should have been enough for me to realize it was time to move on. I was still in a phase of wanting to be free to date whomever I wanted, so this arrangement seemed convenient. He was still struggling with his breakup and I therefore made it clear that I would date as many other people as I wanted and he couldn't say a thing about it. How perfect—or so I thought.

The real problem started when we fell in love and poured our souls out to each other. We both became attached and possessive. Neither of us wanted to get hurt, so we continued our pattern of seeing each other while dating other people. I saw a few different guys and did not sleep with any of them, and he still kept his ex-girlfriend and probably slept with her, even though he would try to convince me that he didn't. He once told me that when he looked at her he saw my face or that when she touched his leg he would get repulsed and wished it were me instead. I was flattered, but felt horrible for this poor girl.

Part of me knew I should not be seeing him and that, no matter what he said, I feared she still thought they were together, exclusively. My feelings for him kept me from breaking it off until I couldn't take it anymore. We traveled together constantly, enjoying the finest of everything, and falling deeper and deeper in love. He began to talk about spending the rest of his life with me, telling me I was his dream girl. I loved hearing it, but at the same time, it scared me. This is a proven liar, something I cannot tolerate, and now he's talking marriage. I was picturing a life with him and liked what I saw. He wanted me to get to know his sons and asked me to go on a trip with all of them. This was too scary. I need to back off, I kept thinking.

I began to see a pattern. We were inseparable on trips, yet when we were in Atlanta we saw each other sporadically and almost never on the weekends. I justified it on the basis of my initial rule that Atlanta was business and travel was pleasure, but I was beginning to believe it had more to do with the ex-girlfriend. He always felt as if there was nothing he could do in Atlanta to impress me and consequently avoided me—or so I thought. As I began to wise up, I realized I was being treated like a mistress. I showed an interest in moving to New York, Miami, or Las Vegas and he encouraged it. He told me he too wanted to leave Atlanta and would move wherever I did. I needed to rent or sell my condo in Atlanta in order to afford a home elsewhere, so Richard offered to cover my expenses in Atlanta, enabling me to move right away. I turned him down, of course. He spoke of how much more we'd see each other in another state where there's more to do. I began to feel that his desire for me to move was a way for him to continue seeing the girl in the building without losing me in the process. He would then be free to visit me as often as he wanted without fear of getting caught and losing her.

I was as much to blame as he was for our dysfunction. I told him outright that we did not work together in Atlanta. I meant that because we didn't do much together. I couldn't commit to a man I only saw once a week or on vacation. He understood it to mean that I didn't enjoy his company here. He thought he had to shower me with lavish trips and gifts to keep my affection when all I really wanted was his time. I admit those things impressed me in the beginning, but once I fell in love with him, none of that mattered. I am notorious for saying the opposite of what I mean. I guess I'm afraid of being vulnerable. I pushed him away almost nonstop.

I justified dating other men and rubbing his nose in it because he was still seeing his ex-girlfriend and that other woman. Feeling as if I was involved with an unavailable man, I broke things off. In the few days we were apart I agreed to go to Las Vegas with another man. The day after I made those plans, Richard convinced me to go to lunch with him to talk about us. Over a glass of champagne, he asked me to go away with him again. I had to decline, telling him I'd be out of town. He was clearly devastated. He always wanted the details of my other affairs and I always obliged. This time was no different. Driven to win me back, he took me home and made love to me for hours.

The next morning I packed and was waiting for my driver to arrive when Richard asked me to come see him. I reluctantly went up to his condo, knowing what I was getting myself into. He took off my skirt and pleasured me, as only he knows how. He went back to my condo and carried my luggage to the elevator. He was shocked that he was helping to send me off to another man and told me that he hates me and that he loves me. I felt the same way. I went downstairs and was whisked away to the airport to meet my date. This was our first date so I knew nothing would happen between us, but I still felt a little guilty.

Richard left for L.A. the day I came back to Atlanta. He told me he was meeting with an investor for a few days and would either return as soon as he was finished or would meet me in Las Vegas if I were up for it. Thrilled to retreat with him on another wildly romantic getaway, I gladly accepted. I arrived several hours earlier and had to check in to the room. Feeling a little bitter about the fact that he brought another woman here after me, I decided to investigate. I knew the room number where they stayed and asked to see the floorplan. Richard told me they had adjoining rooms; nothing like the two-room penthouse we shared. I studied the floorplan and realized he had lied again. It was indeed a two-room suite and larger than the one we had. I was fuming. I asked to see the floorplan of the room he booked for this trip and it was the same as the one he had with her. I didn't know whether I should accept it or not. Mentally exhausted and frustrated, I relented.

I unpacked and ordered room service, pacing like a caged lion waiting to pounce. I was furious. I ate my food, sipped my champagne, and chatted with a girlfriend, plotting his demise. Determined not to spoil my weekend, I tried to let it go. I couldn't. He called from the limo an hour away from the hotel to make sure I got in okay and I let him have it. This man brought the fiery side out of me like no one else has. Sadistically, I enjoyed it. I melted as I saw him walk through the door. I punished him, but more out of fun than anger. We had a fantastic evening as we always did when we were away together.

The next morning he came into my room, telling me we had to go to L.A. because something went wrong with his business there. I immediately started packing my bags, happy to go with the flow. When it comes to my guy's business, I am nothing but supportive. Thirty minutes later he came back into my room to tell me what was really going on. It turns out that his older female friend went out to L.A. when he did in order to get a chemical peel. He helped select a recuperative facility for her and unfortunately they weren't taking proper care of her. She kept calling him in pain, asking him to help. Riddled with guilt, he didn't know what to do. I was amazed. He had lied to me yet again. He told me point blank he was going out to L.A. alone to meet with an eccentric millionaire art dealer who is a potential investor for the project we were working on. Every time I talked to Richard while he was out there, he described the dinners and lunches he had with this guy. In reality, he never even met with him. He was there to help his friend get her treatment and didn't want me to know. I told him to go back and help her, but that I was going home. Not wanting to leave me, he decided to remain in Vegas with me and let the doctors take care of her. The rest of the day was pretty much shot. I was irritated and disappointed and he was worried and guilty. Every time I turned around he was lying to me. Why?

Our trip ended and we went back to our normal Atlanta routine. I would go out with friends or on dates and he would stay to himself, doing who knows what. He asked me to join him for dinner at Chops on a Wednesday. I agreed, but under one condition. He had to come to my door to get me and leave through the front lobby, taking my car, which he would drive. I was testing him to see if he was still hiding me or not. He was adamant that he was not seeing anyone else, but his actions always told me differently. He was acting quite nervous when he got to my place and stayed that way for the remainder of the night.

We enjoyed a fabulous meal prepared especially for us by the chef, a brisket that wasn't even on the menu. The conversation focused on my plans to move, making me a bit uncomfortable. Richard seemed anxious for this to happen, despite my reservations. On the way home I told him again that we don't work as a couple in Atlanta. He said he knew, that I already told him, and that was why he wanted me to move before it was too late. We made love that night and it was great, as always. As I was leaving, he kissed me and whispered, almost under his breath, "I do love you." Somehow I felt this would be the last time we were together and sure enough it was.

I called him the next day to thank him for a wonderful meal, but only got his voice mail. The minute his recording came on, I regretted this act. I knew better than to call a man, even to thank him for dinner. He didn't return my call, so I went out that night determined to punish him. I didn't hear from him for a few days despite leaving another message. That was enough for me. One day he tells me he loves me and wants to spend his life with me and the next he can't even return my call. Determined to move on for good, I wrote him an Email saying I no longer wanted to see him because I had decided to see another man exclusively. I knew I'd be weak if he tried to get me back, so I said a lot of things I didn't mean in order to make him not want me anymore. I was pretty harsh. Looking back, I realize I could have handled things a lot more maturely.

We exchanged a few hateful, hurtful Emails and then quit communicating. I moved on to dating like a champ, but never quite forgot my feelings for him. It's amazing how someone can treat you badly, yet you are still drawn to him. Over a month later I found out what I always feared was true. He never broke up with his girlfriend in the building and was in fact still seeing her. I wondered if she knew about me and, if she did, how she felt about it. I hate the fact I dated a man with a girlfriend. It's completely against my beliefs, yet deep down I knew it was a possibility. I'm also angry with him for putting me in that situation, but angrier at myself for allowing it.

The morale of this story is to always follow your instincts—not your heart. Had I left at the first sign of lying, I would have saved myself a lot of time and heartache. Things got pretty ugly between us in the end, as they do with most passionate short-lived relationships. He was mad at me for seeing other men, something that was hard for me to swallow, considering that he had a girlfriend the entire time. His theory was that mine were new and therefore exciting and his was old and fading. Warped sense of fairness, if you ask me.

This was the final straw for me in my experiences with dating liars. I am now committed to myself, and never allow someone in my life who doesn't treat me with respect and honesty. I may go out with someone a few times, even though I sense he's a liar, but that's just for my research. I'm taking one for the team, ladies, and passing the information on to you.

I still wonder why so many men become involved in exclusive relationships and then cheat. Why don't they do what I do and tell the girl they're seeing other people. That way she can decide if she still wants to date the person and he can go about his business without lying and guilt. I believe the main reason men cheat is because they want the security of a relationship and the fun of an affair without worrying that their girlfriend is doing the same.

As far as the other subject in the chapter title, women gossip, duh!

Photography: Skylar Reeves
Hair: Brandon Darragh
Makeup: Olivia Johnson

The Mind
of a Player

Cracking this egg has proven to be more challenging than making it through puberty, starting my businesses, being an employer and a wife, and surviving the Middle East. Getting to the root of what makes a "player" tick took becoming one myself. Yes, I admit it. I am now a bona fide player. The best way to explain why is by using a narcotics agent as an example. In order to get close to his mark, the officer has to walk a fine line between using drugs for work and using them for pleasure. I too had to change my ways so that I could understand my subject and in the process lost who I truly was.

I took on many characteristics of a player in order to better comprehend that mind-set. I am a one-man woman by nature, yet I had to force myself to date multiple people. A true player does not commit to one person; he or she always keeps their options open. That's a given, but what truly makes one player stand out from another is their methods. Does he chose to lie to get what he wants or does he take the honest approach, knowing she'll put up with just about anything he dishes out. I dabbled in a bit of both, just to see the different reactions.

When I first go out with a guy, I tell him up front that I'm dating several people and do not want a relationship at this time. I also tell him that as long as I'm dating more than just one, I'm sleeping with none. It is absolutely entertaining to see what a man will say to change your mind. Usually the guy is the one running from commitment, but, when the tables are turned his curiosity and ego are aroused. A man cannot stand to be second to another man and will go out of his way to win you—not always because he truly cares for you, but rather to prove to himself that he can.

I experimented with dating more than one man in a day, sometimes even having three dates. It's exhausting and also very strange. I can't possibly connect with someone, knowing two other men are waiting in the wings for me to charm as well. I understand why some people do enjoy it though—it's empowering. You don't worry about getting hurt because you won't get close enough for that to happen. I find it terribly lonely. I adore being intimate with someone, not just on a physical front but emotionally connected as well. I want to wrap myself around the one I'm with and enjoy every inch of him.

Dating multiple people can be extremely tricky, even for the most skilled of players. You may be on the honesty program, but that won't eliminate awkward moments. I was on a date with a man when we ran into a woman whom he's also dating. She knows they aren't exclusive, but felt hurt just the same. She called him the next day to tell him she couldn't see him anymore because she realized she felt more for him than he did for her and the thought of seeing him with another woman again was too much to bear. That's the risk you run of being a player—losing someone you like. I guess if you're truly into someone, you won't let her get away. And if the one you're with lets you go, maybe they just weren't that into you.

I've seen many women try to win the heart of a player. We fool ourselves into believing that we will be the one he changes his ways for. Part of me thinks you can't and shouldn't change someone. If you are dating a man who won't commit to you and chooses to see other women, leave him, if it bothers you. If you don't mind and are doing the same, you may not get hurt, so go ahead and enjoy. There is nothing you can do to make him change. In fact, the harder you try, the harder he'll resist. If a man falls in love with a woman, he will do everything he can to win her heart. You won't have to convince him of it—he will do it naturally.

A lot of men and a lot of women just aren't ready to be in an exclusive relationship. Sometimes we just need to enjoy being single and independent, free to make our own choices and be a little selfish if we want. For some people, this lasts a few weeks; for others a lifetime. I know men in their sixties who've never been married and have absolutely no desire to be. They may unjustly be labeled players when in reality they just don't care. Don't let me give credit where it's not deserved. Many self-proclaimed players choose to live that lifestyle and make no apologies for it.

I was at the Ritz Carlton one evening talking to a wealthy older gentleman who was downright proud of dating as many women as he could all his life. Now in his late fifties, he is considering settling down yet is frightened of the idea of just one woman. I hate to say it, but he may just want to remain on his current path of bachelorhood. He probably doesn't have it in him to be faithful, so he shouldn't try. The other obstacle he faces is his fear of "sharing the wealth" because he has a lot of money. I hate this mentality. If a man falls in love and marries someone, the last thing he should be focusing on is his financial fortune. He should relish the chance of finally finding a partner to share his life with, someone who can enjoy his good fortune with him. If he has fears, he may not have the right person.

A similar phenomenon happens to women. We are afraid to commit to one man and not have our needs met. How often are we swept off our feet, sacrificing everything for the love of our life, only to be let down by this same man? He puts forth an amazing amount of effort, showing you a side of him that is irresistible and making you fall crazy in love with him. As time goes by and you commit to him, giving him everything he wants, he gets comfortable, and slowly takes you for granted. The roses that used to come once a week now come once a year. The love letters stop and the sweet things he used to tell you have gone from "You are so beautiful" to "Hey, how's it going?" Now you're trapped. You're in love with him and want to be faithful, but your soul yearns for the romance you thrive on, the romance that won your heart in the first place. I don't think a woman is too concerned about sleeping with only one man the rest of her life. I think she just wants to know that he won't change once he has her. Face it, no matter what we do, the drive to win us goes away once the challenge is over. We've all seen it firsthand. You finally get fed up and decide to leave. Faced with losing you, he's motivated to kick it up a notch to win you back. You feel loved and appreciated and decide to stay. Days, weeks, maybe, if you're lucky, months later, he falls right back into his complacent pattern. It's unstoppable. We're now becoming conditioned to threaten to leave our man in order to get the attention we so desperately crave. It works over and over, but we gradually lose interest in the game. Trying to manipulate someone into appreciating you is not exactly romantic.

I know many, many female players. In fact, one of my closest girlfriends is a bigger player than any man could ever hope to be. She is confident, gorgeous, and loves attention from men. Torn between her lust for single life and her desire to be in a loving relationship, she plays the game like a champ. Just when she feels herself falling for someone, she snaps out of it, realizing she's just not ready to be tied down to just one man. It's very enlightening to watch her behavior, as it is so much like that of a man—a male player that is. She and I analyze what a guy says or does, comparing it to what we do. For instance, if a guy says he'll call you the next day and four days go by instead, what does that mean? We look at our own behavior and get the answer every time. If we take several days to call someone back, we are either playing the game aggressively or simply not that into him.

She also juggles men like a pro. We were sitting at a local restaurant and bar, having drinks with a guy, John, whom she met the night before. I glanced up and saw David, a guy she went out with the week before, standing at the bar, looking her way. I told her he was here, so she went over to talk to him, leaving me to babysit John. She stayed away thirty minutes, chatting it up, smiling, and being coy, all in front of bachelor #1. Finally, she came back, relieved me of my duties, and picked up where she left off. Not a word or question were muttered about who the other guy was. I was amazed. She pulled it off and didn't even have to explain herself.

This is a common occurrence in her world, giving her the necessary experience to carry it off easily. Men have a harder time with this because a girl is not going to let her guy's talking to another woman in front of her slide. He'll be berated with twenty questions: "who is she, do you think she's pretty, you want to sleep with her don't you?" Come on, ladies. How is he supposed to answer those loaded questions? Don't give him the satisfaction of seeing that he got to you. Simply ignore him and his silly little conversation with another woman. Have enough confidence to know you have nothing to fear. He'll eventually show you more respect and, if not, dump him.

How do I spot a player before I get involved with him? There are some telltale signs. Different women approach him every time you go out or his phone rings constantly and he doesn't answer it. Now, I will observe that it would be rude for him to answer his phone while he's with you, so this isn't always the act of a player. If he takes his phone with him to the bathroom or hides it from you in a drawer, he just might be a player. Some people make no apologies for their lifestyle and will openly flirt with others in front of you or talk about their other affairs. I find this distasteful and suggest that you move on. It's okay for him to play the field—just do it out of your sight.

I was casually dating a guy who was without a doubt a devout bachelor. His success and wealth kept him from letting a woman get close to him; plus I believe he doesn't really enjoy the company of women except for one thing—sex. He is content spending his time building his company, playing golf, and being with his buddies. I don't blame him for that; it sounds pretty healthy and well rounded. (That he doesn't relate well to women is a fact, not necessarily a choice.)

He brought me to one of his company's anniversary parties and acted like less than a gentleman. His friend, who rode with us, opened my door and basically looked out for my needs all night while my date made the rounds, talking to everyone but me. I will grant him the fact that he owns the company and therefore should mingle, but a true gentleman would have taken me by the hand and introduced me to the people he was greeting. After all, I was his date for the night and we didn't even have plans to be there. We were originally going out to dinner, but then he remembered the party and asked if I'd like to go. I didn't mind because I thought it sounded like fun. In hindsight, he should have gone alone.

He would check on me periodically, offering to bring me a drink if my glass was empty. Here is where his true colors came out even more. I only drink champagne or red wine, choices he knows very well. He asked me what I wanted to drink and I of course told him champagne. I had been drinking that all night—why change now? He disappeared for forty minutes, returning with a glass of white wine and telling me that he had been to three bars and none had champagne. I graciously accepted his offering, took a sip, and put the glass down. I'd rather drink battery acid than cheap white wine. He noticed that I no longer had my drink and I simply reminded him that I don't care for white wine. Later that night I was standing by the bar with his group of friends when one of them asked me if I wanted a glass of champagne. Sure enough, there was plenty of champagne available at the inside bar. My dear date went to one outside bar where he was told that they only had champagne inside and not wanting to stand in line, he opted to bring me white wine. I don't mean to come off as looking spoiled in this story. The reason I was annoyed is not the lack of champagne but the lack of initiative and consideration from my date. I gave him a hard time, in fun of course, telling him that he's lazy. He couldn't accept that term, but was okay with indifferent. That was it. We established that he was indifferent to women.

We had a nice dinner with another couple, friends of his, after the party. Not a moment of romance the whole night. We got into his car and he asked what time my curfew was, implying he'd like me to go home with him. I looked at the clock and simply said that it was now. He brought me back to my car and I left with every intention of not seeing him again. It amazed me that he would think I would go home with him after such an evening. If he is so indifferent to me that he can't stand in line to get me a glass of champagne or have enough respect not to flirt with every other woman in the place in front of me, how could I possibly want to be intimate with him?

Here's where I had to make a decision. Should I not grant this player another date or should I stick around to see if he acts like the gentleman I know he can be? My ego can't stand the fact that I don't have him wrapped around my little finger, so I decide to give him another chance. Really, I want a shot at winning him over, just to see if I can. Some players are harder than others and this one is definitely proving a challenge. I have a few tricks up my sleeve, so he better watch out.

I highly recommend that you don't follow my example on this one. What I'm doing is silly. I should put him and his bad behavior in the trash and not give him the pleasure of my company ever again. I don't always follow the rules of dating, even when I know I should. Do you find yourself doing the same? You know you shouldn't call him but you finally come up with a good reason, only to regret it the minute his voice mail picks up. Or you catch him in a lie, but let it go so you can still date him. Why do we do this? We know better. I bet if we stuck to our convictions and moved on every time a man treated us badly, we'd one day meet a great guy. We're wasting time on the bad boy when the good guy is right there in front of us.

Another way to spot a player is by his schedule. If he sees you once a week, there's a good chance he's also seeing many other women. If he sees you five times a week, he has a lot less time for other women—although it's still possible. I was seeing five guys, one almost daily and the others once a week or every two weeks. The hardest part in being with someone a lot is keeping it casual. If you start sleeping with them, it becomes almost impossible. A man thinks this way too, which is why he'll limit how often he sees you. A male friend told me he doesn't see a girl more than once, maybe twice a week because he doesn't want her to get attached. This is sad, but true. He has sex with three different women every week, taking none of them out to dinner or anywhere else. When asked why, he says he's not interested in any of them for a relationship and doesn't see the need to put forth time or effort, but feels they're good enough to have sex with.

Don't let yourself fall prey to this kind of guy unless that's what you're looking for. Some women find that they are sexually interested in a man, but don't enjoy him outside the bedroom. If that's the case, let him know where you stand and just enjoy. There's also the case of great in bed, fun to be with, but not marriage material. You know he's not for you long term, but can't stand the thought of letting him go just yet. Welcome to player status. You continue to date him while searching for your soul mate. I think that's fine as long as he knows to cage his heart and you don't end up falling for someone you know is not right for you. It's hard to not grow attached to someone you spend a lot of time with—be careful.

If you want to dish it out, you better be able to take it. My girlfriend and I find ourselves getting mad at a guy's behavior and then laugh about the fact that we're doing the same thing. She was casually dating a guy and as she began to get more and more attached to him, she found herself questioning whether he was seeing other women and wondering what he did when he wasn't with her. Her mind wandered, driving her crazy. I reminded her that she's dating four other men, so technically she shouldn't be upset with him if he's seeing other women. She laughs and agrees, feeling a bit better. We're no different from men—we want our cake and to eat it too. How great would it be to date as many men as you want, knowing they aren't seeing anyone besides you?

Is there a difference between a player and someone who is casually dating? I think you should be able to date without committing to one person and not be labeled a player. Dating is meant to be fun and explorative. How else are you going to know whom you click with unless you "try men on" until you find the perfect fit? If you jump into a relationship after every first date, you may spend a lot of time trying on the wrong man. The term "player" has a negative connotation, implying someone who lies. I am quite up front about my intentions and determined not to hurt anyone; players typically hide their motives to get what they want without consequences. Treat people well and you will reap the rewards of your actions.

Dirty Girl

This chapter is not for the faint of heart or judgmental prude. It is not politically correct or censored, so proceed with caution. You are about to get an education on how to become every man's fantasy.

We already know that a high-maintenance woman is gorgeous, intelligent, well rounded, and everything a man could want, but let's not leave out the one trait that means the most to him—she's a sexual Goddess. It doesn't matter how good-looking you are or how much money you have, if you aren't great between the sheets, all is lost. To truly be "the whole package," you have to knock his socks off in bed.

I am a very sexual woman, loving everything about sex and romantic exploration. My personal choices are my own and not for you to adhere to, so please do what pleases you. Whether you want to sleep with multiple partners or just one, that is for you and only you to decide. I no longer believe that a woman has to conform to what society demands; she should find her comfort zone and feel good about it. I choose to have only one sexual partner and have never had a one-night stand, not because I feel there is something wrong with it but because I personally don't feel an attraction to a person that fast and therefore know I wouldn't enjoy it. It's purely selfish. I know I could enjoy having multiple partners, but out of respect for my health choose not to. I also think it would diminish the connection you have when you're

Photography: Skylar Reeves
Hair: Brandon Darragh
Makeup: Olivia Johnson

only sleeping with one man. I've never tried it, so I guess I can't say for sure. Knowing my personality, that's my story and I'm sticking with it.

For you really dirty-minded people, let me clarify what I describe as multiple partners. I don't mean more than one man at the same time, although to each their own. I mean sleeping with more than one man whom you are dating. For instance, you sleep with date #1 on Tuesday and then date #2 on Wednesday. Again, nothing wrong with that; it's just not for me.

Let's get to it. Do you know how to absolutely astonish a man in bed? Is it possible you think you do, but he doesn't? How many guys are positive they are the greatest lover you've ever had when the reality is they aren't even close? A lot! To be a good lover, learn what pleases him. I take my time getting to know someone before I go to bed with him—this enables me to seduce his mind as well as his body. I enjoy the power I have over a man when I know just what to do to blow his mind. This comes from learning his personality.

Face it, one wrong move and you can turn him off for good, so pay attention to his reactions and body language. If he moves your hands from his face, take it as a hint that he doesn't like that and don't do it anymore. Work your way down his neck to his chest. Run your fingertips across his entire chest stroking his arm from top to bottom and never staying in one place too long. Alternate lightly kissing his neck and behind his ear with gentle nipping. Combine passion with pain, keeping him alert and interested, not knowing what comes next. Keep moving—too much of a good thing becomes boring and he'll quickly lose interest. This sort of foreplay does not have to lead to sex. If I am still in an exploration stage of a relationship, I tell him up front that I will not be having sex with him. That way he can relax and enjoy what I'm doing without feeling like he has to work hard to get me in the sack. He knows it's not going to happen. And I don't change my mind, ever. You are in control of when you will have sex, not him.

Learn as much as you can about sexual techniques and incorporating toys and dress up in your repertoire. A man is easy to please. Simply taking your clothes off and lying on your back will suffice, but it will not wow him. I have read many books on this subject, talked to hundreds of men and women, and ventured into a sex shop or two in the name of education. Challenge yourself to learn something new and become proficient at it. Be aware of how the different chemistry and personalities between people will alter what you do and how they will affect someone. One man may love having a woman on top while another prefers standing behind her, bending her over the bed, or better yet, pressing her against the wall. Try a little bit of everything until you find his favorite position. Just don't get into a routine. Switch it up a bit. Couples have a habit of getting straight to what works the longer they're together and forget how much fun kissing and exploration can be. How dull is it to know every move he makes before he makes it? Same with you, ladies. Surprise him with a new move or introduce a fun adult toy.

Despite what they tell you, all men want a dirty girl. How does that song go? "I want a lady in the street but a freak in the bed." It's so true. Leave all your inhibitions at the door and open yourself up to whatever comes to mind. Go online to a few porn sights if you think what you have in mind is too kinky. You will quickly see that you are a saint compared to what's out there. Don't overwhelm your guy with one trick after another—let him enjoy one at a time. You don't want to intimidate him or make him feel as if you're more experienced, so learn how to be innocent while introducing handcuffs and anal beads. This sounds silly, but you can do it. The sheer fact that you have those things will excite him. You don't have to be vulgar with your words.

Dirty talk walks a fine line between hot and not. I personally don't enjoy it that much, but some people can't live without it. If you like it, try a few words and watch his reaction. If he responds positively, continue down that path and get as descriptive as you want to. Learn the proper words to use, and more important, not to use in bed. Leave the cute baby talk out. A penis is a penis, dick, cock, etc. You get my point. Don't refer to it as his silly willy, thingy, or pee-pee. Yuck—instant turnoff. And as much as I hate these words, pussy and cunt are appropriate in bed. Some people like the term "make love," while other's skin will crawl when they hear it. Prepare yourself—I'm about to use an offensive word: Fuck. Take a minute and get comfortable with it. Now tell me which sounds hotter.

How do you feel about masturbation? Most men go nuts when you touch yourself for them. I keep eye contact at first, gradually caressing my breasts and slipping a finger in and out of my mouth and running it down my chest while wetting my erect nipple. This can be done with your shirt on or off, depending on how far along you are in the relationship. Not all men savor this. I dated a man who literally could watch me do this for hours. He was in no hurry for his happy ending, therefore he enjoyed hours of my pleasuring him. A different man wasn't fazed by this at all, or so it seemed.

If you are comfortable, venture down your body and delight him with the most visually enticing display of clitoral masturbation. You

Photography: Skylar Reeves
Hair: Sevin
Makeup: Olivia Johnson

can be timid or out-and-out nasty, depending on what you prefer. He likes it all, I assure you. Slip a finger or two in his mouth, then touch yourself between your legs. Repeat this act, but use your mouth instead of his and show him how much you enjoy the way you taste. Caress your inner thighs, teasing yourself and him. This will make him want you to do more. My husband caught a glimpse of me lying on the sofa watching a movie, unknowingly touching myself. It drove him mad and he attacked me, in a good way.

Sorry—I got a bit ahead of myself and left out one of the most important skills you must master: kissing. A good kisser is adored; a bad kisser is ignored. If a man can't kiss, I have a hard time getting past that and quickly move on. He's the same—if you can't kiss, he's out of there. Buy a couple books and practice your technique. Start soft, gradually working your tongue into the picture. Nobody likes a sloppy kisser—or lizards—so don't make quick, darting movements in and out of his mouth. If you encounter a bad kisser, it's up to you to teach him without embarrassing him. Remember on *Sex and the City* when Charlotte was dating a man who would lick her entire face? She tried multiple times to show him what she liked, but finally lost it and told him he was a bad kisser. He was shocked, telling her that's his thing. He truly thought licking a woman's face was sexy. She gave up and ditched him. One day you may have to do the same.

I hate when a guy sucks on my lip too much and almost bruises me in the process. Or when he makes smacking or chirping sounds when he kisses me. What is that? If I hate it, there's a good chance men hate it too, so don't do it. Keep it sensual and passionate. Pull him into you a bit, showing him how much he turns you on. Bring your leg up and wrap it around his. Your whole body should kiss—not just your mouth. I usually wait until I've been on several dates with someone before I kiss him because I don't know how to keep it simple. I am sexually charged and passionate when I kiss a man. His reaction to me, combined with his technique, will either intensify my pleasure or tone it down, giving me a little insight into how he'll be in bed. Isn't kissing fun?

It's time to kick it up a notch. Fellatio is truly every man's best friend. When push comes to shove, his dog will be left out in the cold and his fellatio-performing woman at his feet, literally. There are so many ways to give good head, so try them all. He'll love you for it. Sit him on the edge of the bed, spread his legs just a bit, and kneel before him, taking him in your mouth. The more submissive the position, the better. You can also have him stand with you on your knees. Don't forget to pay attention to all of him. Run your hands up and down his body, alternate between using just your mouth and occasionally your hands in conjunction with your mouth on his penis. Don't spend too much time there with your hands until you're ready to bring him to the point of no return.

Men are visual, so let him see what you're doing. This heightens their excitement. Make eye contact so that he notices how much you're enjoying yourself. The trick is to keep constant motion and contact, learning what amount of pressure pleases him the most—gentle, almost tickling, or extremely hard. The larger the penis, the more sensitive it is, so be careful. Ask him what he likes—better yet, have him show you. I can't imagine he'd tell you no. Don't be embarrassed if you do something that he doesn't care for; all men are different just as all women are. Pay attention and learn from him.

Get creative. Fill your mouth with cold water, letting it surprise him when you put his penis in your mouth. He'll love the sensation. Alternate between hot tea and cold water—not for too long, just a few times. Try blindfolding him and putting different foods on him. Squeeze honey on his penis, then lick it off, letting him taste it in your mouth. Continue with other foods. He'll enjoy the guessing game. Don't use anything that can't go inside you if sex is on the menu for later. Do your research and proceed with caution. Oh, and do keep a warm washcloth close by.

We're now about to get really dirty. Some women are uncomfortable with a man who ejaculates in their mouth or don't mind it but don't want to swallow. A lot of men are offended if you immediately run into the bathroom, spit it out, and brush your teeth—I don't blame them. How would you feel if he did that after tasting you? I'm not saying you have to swallow—that's totally up to you. Just be delicate when you approach this issue. You can easily let it all run out of your mouth and into your hand without his knowing. Curl up next to him and wait for your chance to go to the bathroom to wash up or stretch out on the bed with your palms down, rubbing it in the sheets. See how easy that is. If you really don't want it in your mouth at all, you're going to have to give him a good show to make up for it. You can opt for a "facial"— a real favorite of many men—or ask him to cum on your breasts, telling him how much that turns you on. Everybody wins.

I could talk for hours about this subject, but that's not what this book is about and so let's move on. Cunnilingus, yes please! A man who doesn't like doing this is not a man at all if you ask me. I want every inch of my guy on me and want him to feel the same way. My ex-husband craved every ounce of me inside and out, making me feel completely desired. Unfortunately, all men aren't good at giving head, so it's up to you to teach him what you like. Don't use his head as a steering wheel; instead, gently guide him with your hands or by moving your body until you get him in just the right spot. Move your hips, showing him the speed and pressure you like. A great position that gives you the most control over the movement is having your guy on his back with you straddling his face. Practice and enjoy!

The grand finale: sex. Where do I begin? The title of this chapter is dirty girl, so let me skip over the sweet lovemaking techniques we all know and go straight to the kinky things we all want to know. Fetishes are in all of us. Embrace and enjoy. Play with your alter ego, whomever she may be and tempt his palate. Keep your closet stocked with fantasy fillers, including a little schoolgirl outfit, tons of sexy lingerie, garters (a must), a long blond wig, thigh-high black patent leather stiletto boots with matching wrist cuffs, and a trenchcoat, just to name a few. Wear sexy stilettos to bed as often as possible. There is not one man alive who doesn't like that. Don't incorporate dress up into every encounter—save it to spice things up when they get dull. A sure winner is showing up at his place in a fabulous trenchcoat, boots, and nothing else. It works like a charm and stays engrained in his mind, especially if you keep the boots on when he takes you to bed.

So many positions, so little time. Missionary is powerful and very bonding, not to mention great for the female orgasm. A must-have. One of my favorites is with my guy behind me. There's just something naughty about it, plus it can be done just about anywhere. He can bend you over his desk, bed, or table, put you on all fours, or hold you against a window. Most women won't reach orgasm this way, so incorporate a vibrator or simply let him climax and have him take care of you another way. Speaking of that, what is up with the man who leaves you hanging? I don't think he would like it very much if it were done to him, do you? If your man has a habit of doing this, have him make you cum first, then call it a night. Tell him it's getting late and you need to go home or whatever excuse makes sense. Sweet revenge. I don't need or want an orgasm every time, but it would be nice if he offered.

I love to please my man—what better way than garters and stockings?

If your man is strong, have him hold you up with your legs wrapped around him. That's a nice one. The backwards cowboy is when you are on top facing away from him. A lot of men like this because they can see everything. No matter what position—never forget to touch him. Occasionally wrap your hand around his penis while he's inside you; this adds a new sensation and much-wanted pressure. Slip him into your mouth and then back inside you. A breast man welcomes "titty fucking." Sorry to be so crude, but that's what it's called. Use your mouth on him at the same time if you can reach. One leg up on the table and the other on the floor is fun too. If you're intimidated, buy some books on sexual positions and learn a thing or two. You'll be glad you did.

I almost forgot the "hand job." I dated a man who loved how I did this so much that he would always meet me at the door with a tube of K-Y jelly. I'm exaggerating a little, but not much. He enjoyed this more than anything. I think part of it had to do with the fact that his penis was enormous and extremely sensitive. I could control the movement and sensation a lot more with my hands than with my mouth or body—plus he could watch. This was the same man who liked me to masturbate for him. I'm not going to share my secret on how to do this one; every girl needs to keep a few things to herself.

Here are some interesting stories about sex

I have a male friend who jokes about wanting to open "Handy Houses" across the United States. A guy can finish a round of golf, and, on his way home to his wife, stop off at a Handy House for a quick hand job. I was appalled at first, then realized that a lot of men would certainly go for it. Men don't equate sex with love as women do and have a much easier time justifying cheating on this level. No Handy House will compare to what I can do for my man. Keep your guy happy and he won't think twice about straying.

· · ·

I know a man with a girlfriend who cheats on her with another woman on a regular basis. He knows it's wrong, but justifies it by saying that his girlfriend is sweet and doesn't like dirty sex. Therefore he fills that need with his mistress, who gives the best sex he's had in a long time. How nice for him. Why bother having a girlfriend if she doesn't fully satisfy his needs? The answer is simple. He can't be alone and likes the safety of being with a woman he knows won't stray. He admits he couldn't handle it if she cheated on him. Plus he's intimidated by his mistress's beauty and sexual energy and fears she'd break his heart.

My girlfriend met a man and agreed to go out with him a few days later. They had instant chemistry and made out for hours in his hot tub—naked of course. Knowing he was in the middle of a divorce, she didn't expect anything to come of this and hoped to gain a sexual partner whose company she enjoyed. The next date was great, so she went home with him. They pleasured each other orally, then moved on to sex. He had a very small penis, which she tried to overlook, hoping size wouldn't matter if he knew what he was doing. This poor guy couldn't even keep an erection. He finally managed to get semi-hard and finish what he started, for himself at least. He got up and realized he'd lost his condom—it was still in her. Sad. She went home and used her vibrator. Let's just say that was the end of his chances with her.

This story always makes me laugh when I hear it. A friend of mine went to bed with a much younger man, hoping for a great experience. Halfway through having sex with him, she made him stop, got up, and left. She said it was as if this was his first time and he was trying to copy what he saw in a porno flick. I can't imagine how he must have felt at that moment when she left without an explanation. Ouch.

Another dear friend of mine, a man from South Africa, was dating like a champ, averaging four blind dates a week. We would work out together during the day, and he entertained me with his sexual exploits. I will never forget the story of him in the bathtub with one of his fair ladies. He had lit candles all around, very romantic. She was pleasuring him, when suddenly her hair caught on fire. His eyes were closed and he didn't notice her hair ablaze until he smelled it. He grabbed her head and dunked it under water, putting out the flames. She never saw him again.

Here is a good example of why it's good to know your sexual rating before you open your mouth. My girlfriend was having sex with a guy who kept asking if he was the best she ever had. She thought about it and replied: no, not even close. To make matters worse, he asked if he was the biggest. Again, no. Why go there? There's always going to be someone bigger or better—let's not remind her of it. Ladies, the last thing a man wants you to do is inquire, "How was it" right after sex. If it was great, he'll tell you. If it wasn't, do you really want to know?

Learn from these examples about what not to do. With a little finesse and common sense, you will avoid embarrassment or ending up in someone's joke book. Don't be paranoid about it, though—I'm sure you're a sexual Goddess, leaving a wake of men in your path, full of fond memories of their time with you. Good job.

Travel in Style

A true high-maintenance woman loves adventure and excitement and makes travel a high priority. To land the man who will show you the world, you have to look and act the part. You should have on hand everything you need for traveling in style: great luggage, including an elegant carry-on bag for those overnight trips; professional name tags made for a sharper image; ear buds for movie watching on the plane. This shows you are no stranger to flying and come prepared. You also will need a current passport that you use when checking in, even on domestic flights. This plants the seed that you are an international traveler. And of course, don't forget the business card of your favorite driver at home as well as at your destination, letting him see that you are no stranger to luxury.

I have accumulated these things from years of traveling abroad as well as domestically, upgrading as I go. I have Tumi luggage, Sony ear buds, three passports, and a stack of driver's cards, all of which I constantly put to good use. Travel as much as you can and you will become quite a pro at moving fluidly from place to place, adjusting to time changes and climates with ease. It used to take me days to cope with the five or six-hour time difference when I traveled to Europe, but now I barely notice it.

Become familiar with currency exchange rates and types; this will prepare you for unexpected invitations abroad. You will feel more confident if you know what you're doing, especially if you're traveling alone. There are times when my date asks me to meet him at a vacation spot if he's away on business and can't escort me personally. I am totally at ease in navigating airports, transportation, and accommodations, therefore I can accept the invitation without fear. He usually will make the arrangements and forward the details on to you. Ask if he'll be sending a driver or if you should arrange for your own transportation. A true gentleman will make sure you are safely transported to the airport; the cost is between $65 and $100 and worth every penny. Traveling in style means arriving in a limo, not a cab or, worse, your own car.

Your driver will let you out at the door, and give your luggage to a sky cab, and you never touch a thing. Just be prepared with tip money. Now you simply show your passport at the check-in gate where you will be given your boarding pass with a first-class seat, depending on the man. If you don't know which class he booked you in, you may want to use the regular line versus the first-class one to avoid an embarrassing scene. Proceed to the first-class lounge, if you have access, and sip champagne while you wait for your flight to board.

Upon arrival, a driver from the hotel should be waiting for you at the baggage claim or sometimes outside the gate. Be sure you or your date arranged for this service ahead of time. The driver will collect your luggage for you and whisk you away in a limo, or my favorite, a big, black S-class Mercedes. I usually opt for a Mercedes over a limo as I find it more comfortable and a little less "look at me." Let the bellman handle your luggage and proceed to the check-in counter. If you are arriving before your date, it is up to you to check-in, which is sometimes difficult, especially if the reservation is on his credit card, which it should be. You may need to get him on the phone to verify that you are authorized to check-in for him and they may even require a credit card at that time, so be prepared with one of your own. Just make sure they change the card to his on his arrival to avoid any charges to your card.

If your date gets there ahead of you, have the front desk ring his room to notify him that you've arrived. It would be in bad taste to just go up to the suite unannounced. Here is where things get a little complicated: the sleeping arrangements. A man will likely invite you on a trip in order to speed up the dating process, often hoping to get you in bed sooner than later. I have learned to set boundaries up-front to avoid sexual expectations. I let the guy know that I require my own room and sex is not on the menu. I have yet to be uninvited because of this request. Some male friends have told me that if they take a girl on vacation, they expect her to sleep with him, even if they've just started dating. If this is the opinion of the man who wishes to take you somewhere, I suggest you decline the offer and hold out for a gentleman.

I think the best way to get to know someone is on vacation, away from daily headaches and interruption, which is why I often accept first or second dates for trips. Just be cautious of who you travel with. Always make sure to have your own money, plane ticket, and, most of all, have someone you trust who knows where you are and who you're with. You have an opportunity to spend quality time together, seeing each other in many different settings, and best of all, having fun. I hate sitting across from someone at a dinner table on a first date. You ask each other the same twenty questions, while boredom sets in.

A three-day jaunt is perfect, especially since you have your own room to escape to. If you need a little space, just go to your room for a while until you're ready to come out and play again. If your suitor can afford it, I suggest a two-bedroom suite over two separate rooms; this gives you both a sense of being together yet the freedom of your own personal space. I have grown so accustomed to this arrangement that I find anything else uncomfortable.

I dated a man that absolutely spoiled me. He always made sure I had my own suite, complete with fireplace and hot tub. He would tip the staff a lot of money in exchange for catering to us, bringing me anything I needed and always keeping my room stocked and clean. Once we were more comfortable with each other, he started getting us two-room penthouses. This was the best arrangement we could hope for, with both of us having privacy yet being just across the marble foyer from each other. I have yet to find a man who knows how to travel as well as this one, but I hope to very soon.

Two recent incidents occurred that were challenging, but at least I learned from them. I went to Las Vegas on a first date with someone and assumed he would book a separate room for me. This is, after all, literally our first date and I was used to my previous suitor always booking me a private suite. I called ahead to make sure extra rooms were available, just in case, which put my mind at ease. Sure enough, when we got there he checked us in, but only had one key. I told him I was normally on the two-room plan, but would agree to share the room if he promised to be a gentleman. He agreed, and we shared a room, but I was not happy. I couldn't believe he thought I would be willing to sleep with him or even share a bed so soon. I guess it's not completely his fault—I should have followed my own rules and made my preferred arrangements known up front. Do that many women sleep with men so fast? I suppose so, or it wouldn't have occurred to him that this was acceptable. It was just one night, so I decided to go with the flow and hope for the best.

The date was fabulous. We went to dinner and then a concert, followed by drinking champagne and playing blackjack. I stalled as long as I could and now it was almost six in the morning, our time, so we made our way upstairs. I usually sleep in the nude, but luckily I brought along a little negligee. I slipped away to the bathroom to change and, much to my horror, the negligee was completely see-through. This is definitely going to give him the wrong idea, but I had no choice—wear this or nothing. I crawled under the covers and turned the television on, hoping to convey a totally unromantic mood. He came to bed just in his underwear and before long I think the underwear came off. We chatted for a minute, then I turned the lights off and said how tired I was, expecting that we'd just go to sleep. He curled up behind me, spooning, and made his move. I was able to keep control of his hands and pretended to fall asleep. It had nothing to do with him. He's great, but I was just not comfortable being that close to someone I don't know very well. The only reason I agreed to this arrangement was because I knew his brother and enough about him to feel safe. He was also a very prominent figure. Please use caution when traveling with a man whom you barely know.

Afraid to move an inch and wake him up, I laid completely still for hours, wide awake. I was so uncomfortable that sleep was not an option. I couldn't take it anymore, so I got up and took a shower. I went downstairs to a café to have breakfast and kill time. Many hours passed before I went back up to check on my date. He was sleeping soundly until I accidentally woke him with the sound of my packing. Poor thing, he thought I wanted to leave early, but I was just filling time until the hotel came to life. We had a great time together that day and then headed back to Atlanta. I learned a lot from this experience: always make your intentions clear before accepting an invitation to go on a trip with someone. Surprisingly, he didn't hate me after this. He might have thought me a bit odd, but we've gone out several times since then, so I guess it wasn't so bad for either of us.

The other incident was on a trip to New York. The man who invited me was someone I'd met recently and been out with once. We got along very well and had a lot in common, including a love for travel and the theatre. He asked me to accompany him to New York to celebrate our birthdays and to see his favorite play, *The Phantom of the Opera*. I hadn't been to New York in a long time and I found him interesting, so I accepted. I made it clear that I would require my own room, which he had no problem with. He told me that this trip was about enjoying each other's company and hanging out in a great city, not about sex. I was relieved and eager to go. We went out once more before the trip, getting to know each other a little better and discussing our plans for New York. He asked if I would be comfortable with the Presidential suite at the Ritz Carlton, assuring me I'd have my own room and he'd have a separate place to sleep. I was reluctant, not knowing where he would sleep other than the couch in a one-bedroom suite, but agreed nevertheless.

Upon arrival, I realized there was only one bathroom in the suite and it was located in my bedroom. Luckily, there was a powder room in the foyer for him to use (except for showering of course). I do not like sharing my space with someone I don't know, especially my bathroom. I like to get ready in the morning or prepare for an evening outing in private, listening to music and comfortably going through my routine. The last thing I want is taking turns using the shower or sink. So unromantic. I have nothing to hide and am very comfortable with myself without makeup and my hair not fixed, but I just think it has more impact when I come out fully ready for him. I like it so much that I've decided to always have my own bathroom, even when I remarry. I think it will help keep a little mystery in the relationship.

When it came time to unpack, his initial reaction was to want to unpack in my room. Sensing my discomfort, he placed his clothes in the foyer closet, except for some things he wanted to put in one of my dresser drawers. I wasn't trying to be rude, but I had made it clear that I needed my own room and I wasn't prepared to share. I suppose he thought I meant just for sleeping, but what I meant was for my own space. I like to wake up early sometimes or sleep later without having to worry about disturbing another person—an additional reason why I like my own room.

We moved past this uncomfortable moment, unpacked, and got ready for our dinner reservations. We were running late due to flight delays and only had twenty minutes to get showered and dressed. I showered first and then let him use the bathroom, waiting to get back in so I could finish getting ready. This is why I need my own bathroom. We ended up being almost forty minutes late, but when you're on vacation you can't sweat those things. The restaurant held the table and everything was great. I enjoyed the dinner and his company very much. Next we were off to the play. Our seats for *The Phantom of the Opera* were fantastic, right in the center. I was sitting next to the president of the lead character's fan club who had seen the play almost 200 times. She was telling us how much she hates it when someone coughs during the show. The lights went down, the production began, and within minutes I started to imagine myself having to cough or, worse yet, get a tickle in my throat. I was surrounded by people on all sides, trapped. My mind began to wander, thinking about all the things that could go wrong. I felt myself getting warm and then hot and dizzy, barely able to keep my head up. My date noticed the change in me and asked if I needed to leave. Not wanting to ruin the show, I declined, but moments later took him up on it. He was great at getting us out of there and just as we were walking out the door and into the lobby, I fainted. He held onto me and went down onto the floor with me. That was the strangest sensation ever. I literally remember everything slowly going black and then waking up as he was helping me into a chair. Within just a few seconds an usher got me to a restroom where I promptly got sick. A woman who worked for the theatre who witnessed me faint kept saying how it was the most elegant thing she ever saw. She was so impressed how we went to the floor so gracefully. I drank some water and felt a lot better, but we decided to return to the hotel instead of back in to the play just in case. I lay down on the sofa and he serenaded me; he's a very talented musician. It was very sweet. Not able to stay awake any longer, I went to bed—alone. He slept on the sofa, no questions asked. To this day I have no idea what came over me. It was either an anxiety attack or a touch of food poisoning. My date was petrified that I thought he had put something in my drink. It hadn't even crossed my mind and I feel confident that he didn't, but I teased him about it the rest of the trip.

The next morning was my thirtieth birthday. He had a dozen roses sent to the room, a bottle of my favorite champagne, and breakfast in bed. He's quite a romantic. After breakfast, we had massages in the room followed by a nice nap. It was the perfect start to my birthday. Well rested and full of mischief, we set out on the streets of New York. We jumped in a cab, opting to leave our regular driver behind in hopes of a more rugged experience. We had him drive us around the city and then drop us off in the Village. We then walked for hours, taking in the sights and doing a little shopping, and then enjoyed a carriage ride through Central Park. At one point we passed a Chinese massage parlor and my very cool date decided to take us in. We both got another massage, the second that day, but this one blew the first one away, hands down. We enjoyed it so much we went back the next day for another round of bliss. The setup was a bit seedy, with small curtains separating each massage table instead of walls. I was lying totally naked on my stomach enjoying the best massage of my life when I heard my curtain open and close numerous times. I think the guy who owned the place kept coming in and out, but I can't be sure. We totally lost track of time after spending the entire day out and about. Not wanting to go back to the hotel, we made our way to Times Square. The rest of the night was as spontaneous as the day; we took in two comedy shows and grabbed a slice of pizza at a hole-in-the-wall. It was great. Finally exhausted and out of things to do, we headed back to the hotel. He asked if he could sleep in my bed if he promised to behave, complaining that the sofa was too short for him and very uncomfortable. I turned him down, not because I didn't trust him but because he agreed to give me my own room, assuring me there was somewhere for him to sleep. I also noticed an adjoining room that he could have booked so I didn't feel bad about making him ride the sofa another night. I'm not completely selfish—I offered to sleep on the sofa myself and give him my bed, but he declined.

The next day was Halloween, so we ventured out for some mayhem. I dressed up as a little schoolgirl that night and we went to the parade in the Village. It was a blast. By the end of the trip my date got a few kisses out of me, but that was all. He behaved like a perfect gentleman and therefore I agreed to see him again. We really got to know each other very well and have built a great friendship as a result. I learned from these experiences that you really must be clear with your intentions and requirements before traveling with someone and stand firm, even with yourself.

I strongly urge you to be at ease and familiar with traveling on your own before you agree to first-time dates with a new suitor away from home. You have to be able to get yourself out of any predicament you find yourself in or you're asking for trouble. A lot of people wonder what I do to get guys to take me on elaborate trips. The answer is simple: I don't—they do it themselves. Through conversations with me a man learns very quickly that I travel a lot and that it's something I enjoy but don't take that seriously. The last thing a guy wants to do is take you somewhere and have you think that he wants to be more serious with you than he does. Many men have the time and money to travel and just want a cool girl to enjoy it with.

Never feel obligated to a man simply because he takes you somewhere—I don't care how much he spends. It's his pleasure to have your company, therefore he should be happy to pay—plus he invited you. And whatever you do, never ask a man to take you somewhere—that's tacky. I dated a man who brought me to L.A. for a week and spent over $14,000 and then to Vegas where he spent another chunk of change, but I never once felt indebted. This trip was followed up with one to New York with a similar price tag and still no obligation. We had a ball together and he was thrilled to provide such a nice experience for us both; he enjoyed it as much as I did.

You do owe the person you're with your undivided attention while on his tab. I was flown down to South Beach where my date wouldn't be meeting me until the following day because he was in Rome and not returning until the day after I arrived. The ticket was coach (strike one) and I had to cab it to the hotel (strike two) but the accommodations were impeccable. He arranged for a two-story suite on the ocean in a very trendy hotel. My room was spectacular, with a living room on the main floor and a master suite upstairs via a spiral staircase. The view from the balcony was amazing. What more could I ask for? Food. The hotel didn't offer room service so I headed down to the pool bar to grab a quick bite. Within minutes, a group at the other end of the bar invited me to join them for a drink, which turned into many drinks and hours of conversation. They were a strange mix—a Wall Street billionaire playboy, a retired quarterback turned music manager, an aspiring model/hostess who only dates rock stars, a woman who could pass for a penthouse model, and a guy who turned out to be Vince Neil of Motley Crue. They invited me to go to dinner and

Enjoying a cocktail with Vince Neil and his friends at the Sagamore Hotel

clubbing with them that night and since my date wasn't arriving until tomorrow I didn't see a problem.

I changed into a gorgeous little black dress and met everyone back at the bar. Vince was staying in the same hotel, so it was easy for us to meet and go from there. Ron, the playboy, picked us all up in his Rolls Royce and we headed to dinner. I was surprised by how many complete strangers came up to Vince, fawning over him because he's a rock star. He was gracious to them all, even though he simply wanted to eat his meal and chat with his friends. From there, we went to a place called Rumi where Vince sang "Girls, Girls, Girls" to us. This group was a lot of fun. We headed to Mint, which was my last stop. They invited me to go to Ft. Lauderdale the next day to be in a video Vince was filming, but I declined. This is where I get to the point of my story—I would have loved to take them up on the offer, but I was there on someone else's tab and committed to spending the weekend with him. I later found out that he sent me out a day ahead to see what I would do, knowing I'd be approached. It was a test and I passed with flying colors.

My date arrived the next day, a bit jetlagged, but eager to spend time getting to know me. He brought me a stunning pair of stiletto heels to wear that evening. My kind of guy! We pulled away in a bright yellow Porsche 911 with the top down and the cool Miami air in my hair. He took me to Azul at the Mandarin Oriental Hotel and tempted my taste buds with great food, but most important, fine wine. He is a true connoisseur of French red wine, knowing just what he likes and not afraid to pay for it. We drank a $3000 bottle of wine and savored every drop. He told me how he went into debt as a college student supporting his wine and champagne fetish. I love a man who isn't afraid to indulge. For me it's shoes; for him wine. Actually, for him it was everything. This guy had ten exotic cars, two homes, one in Atlanta and one in Miami on the beach, plus a wardrobe to be admired, complete with couture and classic pieces. His closet was perfectly organized, showcasing his shoe and sunglass collection that numbered in the hundreds.

After dinner we went to Crobar, where he had a VIP section roped off just for the two of us. The champagne was flowing and the service impeccable. A DJ whom he likes entertained us with some of his favorite music. My date was an amazing dancer. He actually traveled the circuit, finding clubs all over Europe to suit his taste and spent weeks at a time indulging himself. This guy lived a true jet-set life. We were having a great time, but as four in the morning approached I asked him to take me back to my hotel. He had his own home in Miami, so there was no question about where he would be sleeping. He did try to get into my room by using his state of intoxication as an excuse. I let him sober up on the sofa, curling up with him for a few minutes, and then sent him home with just a kiss, nothing more.

The rest of the trip was fabulous, complete with more dinner and dancing, all the champagne I wanted, and, best of all, a romantic picnic on the beach. He was a perfect gentleman the entire time, scoring major points with me. I continued to date him for a month or so then

Photography: Kelly Blackmon
Hair: Sevin
Makeup: Olivia Johnson

ended it abruptly. He had booked an extravagant trip for the two of us to spend two weeks in Rome and Paris for Christmas and New Year's. He bought first-class plane tickets and made reservations at the Ritz Carlton, overlooking the Eiffel Tower. He offered to provide a French tutor for me so I could learn French as he planned to take me there regularly. I was excited about finding a man who really knew how to impress me, but unfortunately I had one problem—I was still in love with my ex-boyfriend. At the last minute I called my Prince Charming to tell him I wouldn't be going on vacation with him and that I wouldn't be seeing him anymore. He tried to change my mind to no avail. I wasn't mentally prepared to sleep with him and I knew that would be expected—rightfully so. Now that I look back on it, I feel terrible. He spent thousands of dollars on the tickets, which were now useless. Out of respect and consideration for your guy, make sure you are definitely willing to go with him before you let him make nonrefundable reservations. I will never accept another invitation unless I am fully prepared to live up to my commitment.

It is fun and exciting to be swept away on incredible trips, so be sure to enjoy it. If anyone makes you feel guilty or tries to make you believe you are taking advantage of a guy, don't listen. That's jealousy talking. You are well within your rights to accept an invitation. Just make your intentions clear up front and be certain you are both on the same page. If he doesn't like your arrangement, he can change his mind, but I bet he won't. After all, a girl like you is hard to find and well worth the effort.

Photography: Skylar Reeves
Hair: Sevin
Makeup: Olivia Johnson

Soliciting a Marriage Proposal

*Y*ou say you want to get married. Do you? First, ask yourself why. Make certain you want what you ask for because you just might get it. Before you decide to walk down that aisle, make a list of what you expect to gain from a marriage versus a single life. If you want children, then naturally this is the right way to go. If no children are in your future, then why get married? I have been proposed to six times, engaged three times, and married twice before the age of thirty. If it's marriage you want, I can show you how to get there. How to stay married I will leave to someone else—I haven't quite mastered that talent yet.

There are many different stages in a relationship when the idea of getting married becomes relevant: the whirlwind romance, the typical one-year period, and the dreaded eight-year-is-he-ever-going-to-pop-the-question saga.

THE WHIRLWIND ROMANCE

It's love at first sight; he's stunning and she's gorgeous—a perfect match. He sweeps her off her feet, taking her away to a remote island where they can get to know each other. They fall madly in love, feeling that destiny meant for them to be together. After a week of frolicking in the sand and making love on the beach, they head home; he goes to his place, and she goes to hers. They miss each other desperately Feeling a passion stronger than anything he's known, he realizes what he must do—he must make her his. He gets down on one knee, holding the most precious ring in the world, and asks his love to be his wife. With tears streaming down her face, she accepts. They get married and live happily ever after—or at least until the euphoria wears off.

Many people find this style of engagement rushed and without consideration. I happen to think it the most romantic and exciting. I know right away if someone does it for me—what do I need years of dating for?

I met a man in Las Vegas whom I chatted with for less than half an hour. I gave him my Email address per his request and that was it (I was on vacation with someone else, so I didn't pursue this any further). He contacted me the following week, sending me poems and beautiful letters. We spoke on the phone a few times and within weeks he flew in to spend a few days getting to know me. By the end of the first day he asked me to meet him the next morning at Tiffany's to pick out my engagement ring. He was serious. I didn't feel the same way, so I declined and we didn't pursue dating any further.

This is a great example of knowing when someone is right for you. He felt as if I was everything he had always been looking for and that fate had brought us together. He really believed that. He almost believed it enough for both of us. My point is that in his mind there was no need to date me—I was what he wanted. I've felt that way about people before; we all have. It's when you both feel the same way that it's right.

If I ever remarry, I want it to be fast and furious. Sweep me off my feet and take me away from all other men. A long courtship makes for an anticlimactic wedding, in my mind. Don't even get me started on living together—why bother? Let's share the bills and housework and maybe one day if we don't get too bored with each other, we'll get married. I'm not on that program.

Now how do you get him to ask soon? It's easy. Don't commit. If he falls madly in love with you, but you won't agree to date only him, he has two choices: accept it and hope you don't marry someone else or ask you to marry him and make you his completely. It's that simple. You both should know right away if you want to spend the rest of your lives together. If you don't, then you should continue dating but keep your options open.

You run the risk of losing him to another woman when you go this route, but you always run that risk. If you won't commit to him, he's free to date other women and in doing so may find someone else. Good. Better now than when you are in a committed relationship, or worse, married. I've known many men with girlfriends who cheat because they didn't feel they're doing anything that bad. "We're not married" or "I live alone" are common justifications.

I'm not saying that this method is for all women, but if it's an adventurous romance and proposal you seek, it just might do the trick. It's worked for me, even though I wasn't trying to solicit a proposal—I was simply keeping my options open. Almost every man I've dated who I wouldn't commit to has asked me to marry him right away or hinted at it. The timid ones afraid of rejection will put it out there, hoping you'll give them a sign that this is what you want too. I don't let them off so easily. If you want to know if I'll marry you, you have to ask.

THE ONE-YEAR DANCE

Sue and Jeff celebrate their one-year dating anniversary Sue hopes Jeff will surprise her with a wedding ring at dinner. They've talked about it, and both want to get married, but when is the operative question. Dinner comes and goes and no proposal. Sue, clearly upset, grows agitated. What is wrong with her, she wants to know? Why won't he marry her? Sue and Jeff have their own apartments, but often sleep at each other's place. She goes out with him whenever he asks and doesn't get in the way of "guy's night out." They have been sleeping together almost since the beginning of their relationship. Enough! I'm bored writing about it—I can't imagine living it. You know where I'm going with this story. Jeff has his cake and he's eating it too—because Sue served it up to him. Why shouldn't he enjoy it?

Ladies, if you've been with a guy for a year and he hasn't popped the question, maybe it's time that you move on. What is he waiting for? He can have a million legitimate reasons, but the bottom line is that he's just not that into you. Sound familiar? Why else would a man risk losing you to another man? You've probably done so much to make him comfortable with you that he is just that—comfortable. He has no real motivation to move forward in the relationship unless he is ready for children. You're always there for him when he needs you and then he puts you back on the shelf until he needs you again. Don't let him do it. Leave. I don't mean you have to stop dating him, I just mean you have to get a life of your own and start seeing other men. He will either wise up and take you off the market for good or he won't. If he doesn't, then good riddance to someone who can't decide if you're good enough to be his wife. Give the guy who will commit a chance at finding you.

THE EIGHT-YEAR SAGA

This will be short and to the point. Don't let it happen—get out while you still have a few good years left.

Common Excuses Men Use To Postpone Marriage
1. I want to graduate college first, then focus on my career. Once I make enough money to support a family, I'll be ready.

   That's a legitimate reason to want to postpone marriage, but what happens to you in the meantime while he's chasing the dollar? You're off the market, waiting for him. Once he's made it, he might decide he wants a new girlfriend. This is common with men whose income level changes—they want to upgrade everything in their lives, including their woman. You've just wasted several of your best years on a guy who has tossed you out like last week's paper. If you really want to get married and feel you're ready, don't wait for the unattainable man. I know you love him, but, honey, this too shall pass. If he's not willing to make you his, why should you make him yours?

2. I'm recently divorced and need to be on my own for a while.

I agree that this statement is true for a lot of people. Many therapists recommend that you take at least two years after a divorce before you enter another marriage. That's great for him, but if you are emotionally healthy and ready to be married, why should you wait for him to sow his oats? Move on.

3. I'm already married, but I am going to leave her for you and then we can get married.

Your first mistake is dating a married man. There is never a good reason to do this. Never. The second mistake is believing one word out of his mouth. The third and fatal mistake is thinking he will be different with you. If he was able to cheat on her, he will most definitely do the same with you. Leave him and never go back.

4. I want to be financially set for life before I get married or have children. That way I know I'll be able to be with my family in times of major illness or tragedy, not to mention everyday life.

I am casually dating a young man with this exact philosophy. He truly wants to be that financially stable before taking on the responsibility of a wife and children. His father missed out on a lot of his youth because he was always at work, therefore my friend wants to avoid repeating this with his own children. I find it commendable, but hardly realistic. He is only twenty-seven with a lifetime of earning potential and bills ahead of him. I'm sure some girl will come along, win his heart, and throw his theory out the window.

HOW TO SCARE A GUY INTO NEVER MARRYING YOU

1. Propose to him. That's just sad; he may say yes at that moment, unsure of what to do, but I guarantee he will change his mind. No man wants a woman to propose to him.
2. Give him an ultimatum. When I tell you to date other men until he asks you to marry him, I'm not suggesting that you issue an ultimatum. Marry me or I'll date other men is not a good approach. I am merely suggesting that you get on with your life. Don't ever approach a man with the topic of marriage. It's his job, not yours. I know a man who was given an ultimatum when he started dating a woman. She told him there had better be a ring on her finger within 365 days or she would leave him. They got engaged. The night before the wedding, he called it off—I can't say I blame him.
3. Buy a wedding dress just in case. That's weird. He'll think you're a bit nutty.
4. Tell all your friends you two are getting married when you're not. He won't find that endearing or cute. He'll be mad and will probably quit seeing you.
5. Talk incessantly about how much you want to get married. Every guy assumes you want to marry him, whether or not you do. They're a bit narcissistic.
6. Mention you want six children. Keep that tidbit to yourself for now. I dated a man who wanted four or more children, so I ruled him out.

MY PERSONAL THOUGHTS

Marriage is a great institution when both people have the same values and ideas on what makes a marriage work and are willing to do that work, but in this day and age of cheating and divorce I wonder if marriage is outdated. Have we evolved to another means of bonding other than marriage? Should we just have exclusive relationships, going from one to the next when problems arise or when we get bored? This may

A Princess Bride

sound ridiculous to a lot of people, but isn't that what we're doing? I have been divorced twice, not as a result of infidelity, but irreconcilable differences. I was raised with the belief that marriage is forever, which is why I stayed in an unhappy marriage for nine years. I tried everything I knew to make it better, but nothing worked. I finally gave up. I have become a statistic more than once. My second marriage ended in less than a year, true to form with the statistics, and supposedly the third marriage will end even quicker.

I must admit that I am a bit old school and love the concept of marriage, therefore I am determined to make the third time a charm. I know without a doubt what I am looking for in a man and will not settle for anything less. Even if I fall in love again and again, I will not marry the wrong man. I encourage you to make a list of all the qualities you look for in a husband as well as those traits you can't possibly live with and hold true to your wants. You will have a better chance at a successful marriage if you marry the man of your dreams versus the man whom you think you can mold into the man of your dreams. People don't change—find the one who's perfect for you just the way he is.

One last piece of advice: if you want a man to ask you to marry him, be worthy of a proposal. Make sure you are a well-maintained woman in high demand and he will seek you out above all others.

Take Him for Everything He's Worth

Shame on you if you who flipped right to this chapter. If you are of the mind-set that a man owes you something, we need to talk. And as for you, guys, get over yourself. Not every woman is after you for your money. On the contrary, many women either have their own money or simply have enough integrity to leave yours alone. Let's look at some examples of dating, divorce, alimony, and child support.

Example 1
I overheard one of my girlfriends complaining about not taking her husband for more money so she could just live off him instead of working. They dated for many years, each attending college and going on to get good jobs, then getting married and buying a condo together. After three years of not-so-wedded bliss, she asked for a divorce. They sold the condo, split the equity and furniture, and agreed on joint custody of their puppy. He makes more money at his job than she does, but that didn't play a role in their divorce settlement. There was no alimony paid to either party.

Okay, ladies, in this example, give me one good reason why he should pay her alimony? I can't think of one, either. This appears to be a fair settlement. She should feel good about doing the right thing by her ex-husband and herself.

Photography: Kelly Blackmon
Hair: Sevin
Makeup: Olivia Johnson

Example 2

I heard a story about a woman who married a rich man. They were both young and attractive and had a good time together when they were dating but things changed after they had been married a year or so. The fights picked up, even getting physical, and their affection for each other changed from love to tolerance. He became a workaholic and she quit her job to become a shopaholic. She felt him slipping away, so she decided to have a baby. She wasn't trying to make the marriage better; she was planning on getting child support once she divorced him so that she would not have to go back to work. I couldn't believe it—that's as low as it gets. Nine months later she divorced him, suing for child support and alimony. The court system obliged, giving her the house, alimony until she remarried, and of course child support for eighteen years. She did it. She got rid of him and set herself up for years to come.

This is wrong on so many levels. She decided to quit working, making her dependent on him. She wanted the baby and took it with her. She divorced him and took what he already had, his house and some of his money. How would we ever find this acceptable? This is why so many good men are afraid to get married. It's not commitment phobia—it's fear of being taken for everything they worked hard for. Can we blame them?

Example 3

Boy and girl meet in college. He's studying to be a doctor; she a biologist. They fall in love, get married, and the girl gives up her dream of becoming a biologist and instead works to put him through medical school. He graduates and becomes an extremely successful doctor. They have two children and a luxury lifestyle, thanks to both of their efforts. They make a joint decision for her to stay home, raise their kids, and take care of the house and of course him. They seem happy—the perfect American family. One day he leaves for another woman. After a bitter divorce battle, she was left with the house, her children, child support, and alimony. Is this fair? No. She gave up her career aspirations for his. He has the education and the ability to make an incredible living while she does not. She may get child support and alimony for a while, but that won't support her forever. If she decides to go back to college and pick up where she left off, the kids will suffer by not having their mom around. If she waits until the kids are grown and gone, she will not have the financial support needed to go to college and work part-time. She got the bad end of this deal. Not only did her husband cheat on her and abandon her, he left her without the ability to support herself. I suppose that's the risk she took when she went along with his plan.

I have been married and divorced twice, doing the right thing each time. In both cases, alimony would have been a reasonable request, but I opted to forgo that luxury. I couldn't stand the thought of being dependent on them, nor did I want to give them bragging rights—"My wife took all my money." No way! Plus I feel great knowing that I have integrity and pride. I asked for a divorce from my first husband after nine years of marriage. He didn't want it yet I did, so why should he suffer. We split our joint assets, property we had worked together to acquire, and I bought him out of my businesses. He kept his company and all rights to his income. I know I could have gotten alimony and more property, but I didn't think that was fair. After all, I made the decision to leave.

The second divorce was mutual and friendly. We had been married less than a year and, due to unforeseen circumstances, could no longer be together. I gave up my career at his request and moved to the Middle East with him so he could take over his family business. Once the decision to split was made, we applied for an uncontested divorce. I left with what I had when I came into the marriage and he retained all rights to his inheritance, company, and money. I did not ask for alimony or any other support. I could have gotten it, considering I gave up everything for a life with him, but I didn't want to go down that road. He was my best friend in the beginning and my best friend in the end—why screw that up for cash? And again, I still have my reputation as a woman with integrity intact.

Society has gotten so skeptical, with men thinking that women are after them for their money and women thinking men are after them for sex. There's a lot of truth to this, which is probably why we think that way. This equation dates back to the beginning of time—the powerful, rich man pursuing the most beautiful woman in the city. Why are we so offended by this? We all want to be valued for who we are inside, not just what we have to offer, whether it's money or sex. But let's get real. A woman seeks security and a man seeks sex. There is the most basic form of sex for money, prostitution. Some may say marriage is glorified prostitution and, to some degree, they may be right.

The question then becomes how do women get their need for security filled, and men, for sex, while maintaining integrity and treating people well? I guess it depends on what you deem acceptable behavior. If paying a woman for sex is okay in your book, then knock yourself out. If you have higher standards and want something more, then try "courting." Remember the days when men would go out of their way to win the heart and body of a woman they desired? I am astounded by how many men think I will go to bed with them on the first date. Just because you bought me a meal doesn't mean I'm going to sleep with you. Put forth some real effort, guys. Plan fun trips and romantic evenings. Once she feels a bit of security with you, she'll happily share her body. I know that a guy can easily get a woman to go to bed with him, even on the first date, but, come on, where's the fun in that? Women, quit being so easy! You're making it harder for those of us who like a good chase.

On that note, ladies, let me ask one more favor of you. Please, quit acting like gold diggers—you're giving the rest of us a bad name. I don't care if you truly are after his money. That's your problem, but keep it to yourself. Hundreds of men have told me stories of first dates with women who tell them they want a big-ass house and a big-ass car and a big-ass bank account. Guess what. He wants his big-ass check and to get the hell away from you.

There are more subtle ways to get your point across. If it's a big-ass house you covet, talk about the style of the home and how you want to decorate it. This will show him the level of lifestyle you are looking for without making him feel he has a dollar sign on his forehead. You can apply the same method for the car and the bank account. Tell him how much you love the Mercedes 500SL and how you hope one day to be able to afford your dream car. He will see how expensive your taste is and weave himself in or out of your life. As for the big-ass bank account, this is a little trickier. I think the best way is to get his opinion on how much money it would take to retire by, say, forty-five. He will freely talk about how much money is needed to support a certain lifestyle, revealing how well he intends to live.

Finding security with a man can be a daunting task. How can we ever be sure that security won't be interrupted? We can't, so protect yourself the best you can. I've always been a leap-of-faith kind of girl myself, but if you prefer to cover your bases, that's okay.

In a marriage, a prenuptial agreement is a tool used to protect both parties in the event of a divorce. You may want to seek the advice of an attorney, outlining what you need in the event of a divorce and drawing up the papers. Get your man to sign before you agree to marry him and you will have protected yourself to some degree. If you intend to get paid if he divorces you, at least he knows up front and can decide to proceed or run.

Some women keep a stash of cash that their husband doesn't know about. This can prove useful if he ever leaves you high and dry. There are many ways to do this without his knowing. Get cash back when you go to the grocery store or salon; it will look like part of the overall bill and he will be none the wiser. Withdraw money from the ATM on a regular basis for "pocket money," but add it to your stash and use credit cards instead. I'm not condoning dishonesty—I'm simply teaching you to have a bit of added security if you need it.

You may love and trust your husband now, but what happens if he turns on you and leaves you with nothing—no job and no money? Plan for the worst and hope for the best. If you are in an unhealthy marriage, you may even consider keeping a lockbox somewhere with cash, a credit card that he can't access, and legal documents (your passport, copy of driver's license, etc.) just in case. We've all heard horror stories—be prepared.

Security in a dating environment is an oxymoron, if you ask me. You may devote yourself to a man, giving him all your time and sometimes your money, hoping that one day he'll ask you to marry him. Years may go by, and then he leaves you for another woman—no note, no explanation. Just gone. There's no security in that.

If you are dating, not married, you may consider keeping your options open and your money to yourself. A lot of people disagree with me, but I strongly feel a man should pursue a woman, paying for their meals and trips. She should pay her own bills and upkeep (hair and nails, etc.) and he should pay for the dates and his own bills. I am a bit old fashioned I know, but most men I date wouldn't have it any other way. They'd think I'm trying to buy their affection if I pay. I used to offer, but, after offending several men, I quit.

Keep your options open—don't commit until marriage. That's an extreme statement, but one I live by. Why should I rule out all potential suitors for a man who is not sure if I'm the woman of his dreams. If he needs time to figure this out, I'm happy to give it to him, but I will not sit on a shelf waiting. I'm going to keep dating, looking for the guy I connect with the most. May the best man win.

Photography: Skylar Reeves
Hair: Sevin
Makeup: Olivia Johnson

Getting What You Want, Wanting What You Have

Loving a person who doesn't love you back can be the most soul-destroying feeling you will ever have. You are helpless to change how you feel, yet desperate to move on. What is it that makes us absolutely yearn for someone we cannot have? Maybe that's just it—wanting the unattainable. Whether we admit it or not, a challenge is difficult to pass up.

Something easily attained is often tossed aside with very little value placed on it, yet whatever is just outside someone's reach is what they strive for the most. That's true of just about anything. If a man catches a woman's eye, but for whatever reason she can't have him, she'll stop at nothing to win him. If someone is on a quest for a higher position in their career, they'll work tirelessly until they attain their goal. The motive behind this drive isn't always a negative, but perhaps an incentive to push you harder than you would normally push yourself. The crucial part is recognizing when to admit defeat and move on to the next challenge—never linger in a no-win situation.

Let's agree that certain types of people aren't worth pursuing at all. Married men as well as men with girlfriends should immediately be ruled out. All is fair in love and war, but I feel strongly about not messing with another woman's man. Another type of man to avoid is the emotionally unavailable one. He will do nothing more than drive you insane—move on. Limit yourself to someone worthy of you and your efforts.

A woman faces many challenges in attaining true love and companionship. She'll unwittingly fall for a man she can't have, or one that she shouldn't be with. She will spend weeks, months, even years, trying to win his heart. Why waste so much time on someone who is not right for you? The sting of rejection is often the force behind this madness. Our self-esteem cannot handle the fact that the one we love doesn't feel the same way. We just know that if we change their mind, we will feel better about ourselves. Look back on your past relationships and recall how you felt when someone broke up with you. How long did it take you to get over him? Now, how did you feel when you ended a relationship? We tend to move on a lot faster when we do the breaking up.

I wrote the manual on seducing the unattainable man and, even though I recommend that you avoid him, I will teach you how to win him over. The most difficult is the case of he-doesn't-know-I'm-alive. Here is an example of a potential office romance. You have your mind set on a man whom we'll call John. You see him all the time, your imagination runs wild, yet he hasn't so much as said hello to you. He works in your office, is single, and drop-dead gorgeous. You must have him, but how? Follow these steps and he'll be begging to go out with you.

To attract John, you have to look fantastic and exude confidence. We'll assume you're a high-maintenance woman, which means you are definitely worthy of his attention—he just doesn't know it yet. Your hunting ground is your office, so make the most of your time there. Dress to impress. Depending on your line of work, I recommend a great looking suit tailor-made to fit your body. Reveal a hint of skin; just don't err on the side of showing too much cleavage. It won't go over well with him or your co-workers. Look elegant and sophisticated, not sexy. Wear your hair and makeup in a professional manner, but not too subdued. A gorgeous pair of stilettos is just the thing to complete your look and get this man's attention. Now that you're the best-looking woman in the office, it's time to improve your attitude.

You must have an air of confidence about you if you are to close the deal. Fake it until you make it, if you have to. Have you ever encountered a person who is clearly intimidated by you? You will have a tendency to walk all over them, intentionally or not. And the last thing you'll do is respect them. Don't be that person. Be strong, determined, yet never arrogant. Know your worth and don't be afraid to show it. Women tend to downplay their qualities and abilities while men openly flaunt them. Women are afraid of coming off as bragging. How is someone to know who you are and what you're capable of if you don't tell them? This goes for your career as well as your relationships. I've never been timid when describing who I am or what I do. I am often judged by my outward appearance, which is why it's so important to me that by the end of a conversation a person realizes I'm intelligent and successful, not just attractive. It's amazing how many men as well as women are astonished by the fact I have a brain. I can't blame them. I too find myself judging a beautiful woman in the same fashion.

A confident woman doesn't apologize for who she is. On the contrary, she is proud of her achievements and comfortable with her mistakes. Having been married twice before the age of thirty, I have two choices when sharing that personal information: be embarrassed and timid, or matter-of-fact and honest. I always go with the latter option, as I have nothing to be ashamed of. I loved two men enough to marry them, but due to unfortunate circumstances those relationships ended. I have grown as a woman from loving them and experienced more life than one could dream of. I never regret and always look ahead—and it shows. If I were apologetic when telling a potential suitor about my previous marriages, he would probably have a negative reaction. Because I am confident about it, this helps him to quickly move past it. In fact, I have yet to receive a judgmental response.

Apply this practice to whatever it is that challenges you. Take the worst thing you've ever done and look at it as an experience that makes you a stronger person today. Don't show weakness or insecurity; you must always exude confidence. Vulnerability is not to be mistaken for weakness. Showing your vulnerable side to a man can be quite endearing. A person must be strong and confident in order to be comfortable with being vulnerable. Men want women to be feminine, even in the workplace. I don't know anyone who likes it when a woman tries to act like a man. You can be professional while still being a lady. This way of being takes practice and determination. Find the perfect balance of confidence, vulnerability, professionalism, and femininity and you will be the most sought-after woman in the office.

You have the look and you have the attitude, now it's time to get the man. You and John have worked together for quite some time, but he has never pursued you. Let's walk through this step by step. Make your presence known. Go to John for input on a project or simply ask his opinion on something you're working on. He will be happy to help, especially if you gently stroke his ego. Tell him how much his opinion means to you, considering how good he is at what he does. Let him know that you've been struggling with this and could really use his assistance. Watch him step into action to help you, which in turn boosts his ego. You just scored huge points without making your personal intentions known.

Always remember: a man does not want a woman to pursue him. He is the hunter and you are the prey. That doesn't mean you can't lead the hunter to the woods; it just means he can't know you're doing it. John now knows you're alive and subconsciously likes you because you made him feel good about himself. Human nature will make him seek you out again to give you another opportunity to compliment him. This is great, but be careful. Too much flattery will make you look interested and possibly desperate. It's too soon for him to know you want him.

Once you've built a friendly rapport, it's time to let him see you as a woman, not just a co-worker. Have a male friend pick you up at the office and take you to lunch. Make sure he comes at a time when John will be there, but don't introduce them. Give your friend an affectionate hug and quietly leave with him. The more subtle you are, the more John will be intrigued. We women tend to divulge too much information. Let a guy's imagination run wild. Picture the two ways this encounter can go. You can introduce John to your friend Bill, making him feel comfortable that this is just a friend. Or you can let him see you with Bill and wonder who he is. Is it your brother, a boyfriend, or simply a friend?

A few days later send flowers to yourself. This seems silly to a lot of people, but it is effective. A woman in demand is attractive to a man. After all, we want what we can't have or, worse, we want what someone else has. The flowers will affirm that Bill is a boyfriend and make John want to win you away from him. Even if John wasn't interested in you before, now he will be. It is now acceptable for you to start an innocent flirtation with John. He won't assume you're into him because he knows you have a boyfriend. However, he will enjoy the flirtation and be drawn to you. Before you know it, John will begin pursuing you.

This is an example of getting someone's attention. What do you do once you have his attention, but can't seem to close the deal? This becomes a lot trickier. Understand that there's a difference between a healthy, fulfilling relationship that comes naturally and a manipulated one. If two people are truly into each other, things tend to flow easily and passionately. There is very little game playing and hurt feelings. This is the type of relationship we should aspire to, yet somehow we take it for granted.

I was dating a man who epitomized the possibility of a healthy, wonderful relationship. He was gorgeous, made me laugh, treated me with respect, and was self-sufficient and responsible. We had an incredible time together, enjoying an amazing sex life and simple pleasures. We went to movies, shot pool, ate out, and exercised together. He liked to travel, as did I. He had a great sense of style, an incredible personality, a heart of gold, and a smile that would make you melt. He was confident, but not arrogant, took me to new and interesting places, and was quite attentive. He enjoyed spending a lot of time with me and was very vocal about his feelings without being a sap. I know—he sounds too good to be true.

Now let me tell you why I could be considered a high-maintenance woman in this scenario. I had the greatest guy in the world. He was crazy about me and I felt the same way about him. Unfortunately, I was destined to break his heart and mine due to my need for luxury. He made a good living and was working at building security for his future; he was ambitious and smart in his financial decisions. The problem was that he and I look at lifestyles in completely different ways. He's happy to drive a Honda while I adore my SL500 Mercedes. One night he made the mistake of knocking people who buy a Mercedes in order to impress others. He wasn't directing his comment at me, but I couldn't help feeling attacked. He looks down on money and living well—I aspire to it. I refuse to apologize for the way I live and the decisions I make, even if it means losing a great guy.

I travel first-class, hiring drivers and staying in five-star hotels. He typically flies on a Buddy Pass and crashes with friends. Neither method is wrong; they're just vastly different. He invited me to go to New York, London, and California, but I never accepted. I wanted to be flexible and easygoing, but I just couldn't stand the idea of sleeping on someone's couch. It's just not what I'm used to or what I enjoy. At times I felt shallow because of it, but, at the same time, I didn't think I should give him the impression that I enjoy this type of lifestyle. In the long run, I thought it better to let him know up front what he's getting into with me versus letting him believe I'm someone I'm not.

You're probably wondering why I dated someone who was so ultimately unsuited for me. I asked myself that same question, daily. I enjoyed his company and, at that time in my life, wasn't looking for a husband. I justified the relationship as a fun fling. The hard part came when I considered his feelings. He was twenty-seven, never married, and definitely looking for a potential wife. I told him on our second date that I was twice divorced, not interested in having a husband or a relationship, and don't believe in "boyfriends." I am either single or married, no in between. He had been warned. It was cute though, because he refused to believe me—he thought for sure that I wanted what he did, an exclusive relationship.

Photography: Kelly Blackmon
Hair: Sevin
Makeup: Olivia Johnson

We had been dating for several weeks, seeing each other almost daily. It was great. I enjoyed his company so much that I quit dating other men, not because he wanted me to, but because I no longer had the desire to. We both agreed not to have sex with anyone else. Everything was wonderful between us until he started pressuring me for a commitment. He told me that his feelings for me had grown serious and that he wanted to know where we were going. I asked that we keep things as they were. We were having fun—why screw that up? I must admit, I was falling for him as well. I just knew there was no future for us and didn't want to get more attached than we already were. I loved so much about dating him, but not about sacrificing certain luxuries that I'm used to. My past boyfriends would take me around the world, wining and dining me, planning fun surprises. I enjoy that and missed it. I never let him know what was on my mind. This level of lifestyle was out of his reach and frankly not of interest to him. I didn't want to make him feel badly for something he couldn't change and I didn't want to be judged for what I liked.

The longer we dated, the more apparent our differences became. I finally faced the fact that we were not meant for each other and ended the relationship. I learned a lot about myself during this time. No matter how much I like someone, I cannot deny who I am and what I want out of life. Had it been years earlier, I would have stayed with him and, who knows, even married him. Leaving him was difficult, but after living through two marriages to the wrong men, I knew better than to stay. This experience reaffirms my belief of being married or single—no exclusive relationships. I was spending all my time with a man I knew I wouldn't marry and therefore missed potential opportunities to meet one better suited to me. Use caution before you commit, and know that if it doesn't seem right, it probably isn't. Be strong enough to walk away from Mr. Wrong and into the arms of Mr. Right.

This was an example of a good relationship that flowed easily without a lot of game playing, yet ended due to personality differences. What do you do when you get a man's attention, but can't seem to get things moving the way you want? There are many different scenarios, so let's examine them one at a time. In a very casual dating environment you will hear from a man as much as once a week or as little as once a month. Remember, he knows that the less he sees you, the less attached you will become. A sure sign of a man's trying to keep it casual is limiting contact. He will call just enough to keep you interested, but never more than necessary. Don't fool yourself into believing that he's quite busy with work and other obligations and this is why he has so little time for you. The truth of the matter is that if a man is truly into you, he will stop at nothing to be with you—a lot. There's always time to call you just to say hello, even when he's busy. Face the music when you hear it playing—no more excuses.

You know the kind of man you're dealing with, yet you still want to pursue him. I wish I could convince you to move on to someone who deserves you, but, if you're anything like I used to be, you won't put him aside until you wrap him around your little finger. My first bit of advice must be adhered to under any and all circumstances—don't call; let him call you. And whatever you do, don't take his call every time. There's no challenge in knowing that whenever he decides to take you off the shelf, you'll be available. You may return his call, but not right away. If you haven't heard from him in a long time, wait at least a week to call him back. Always be friendly when you speak to him and never ask what he's been up to. Let him lead the conversation. Remember, you don't have to answer all of his questions. Keep your whereabouts a mystery. You can easily brush off his probing with a flippant response. If he asks, "So, what have you been doing lately?" You should reply, "Oh, you know, a little of this, a little of that." You answered his question, yet he knows nothing more now than he did a few seconds ago. It'll drive him crazy. This process may take weeks, even months to be effective. Just don't lose hope—it works.

He will perceive you to be a challenge and put you at the top of his list. A lot of my male friends call this the A-List, the girls they are most interested in pursuing. The challenge is finding the right balance between being aloof and showing interest. He will quickly move on if he doesn't feel that you are into him. I find the best method is to be a lot of fun on a date, but unattainable when you're apart. He will love spending time with you and go nuts over the fact that he can't see you more often. One other important piece of advice—never sleep with him during this dance. A man quickly loses interest in a woman once she sleeps with him—that is, unless he's already in love with her or the sex is the best he's ever had. I've dated men for months, traveled with them, never had sex with them, and they still call.

A point will come when you should decide to continue pursuing this man or move on completely. If the chemistry wasn't explosive in the beginning, the attraction will probably fade for both of you. Chasing each other is fun, but it can grow tiresome. If he's interested in you, he will make a move toward dating you more frequently. If not, cut your losses and move on. Learn to recognize the fact that you shouldn't have to play this game if a guy is into you from the start. He will automatically pursue you, stopping at nothing to make you his. Try not to take the way a man reacts to you personally. We are all attracted to someone for different reasons. You may be gorgeous, successful, and funny, but he chooses someone plain instead. That's not a knock at you. He's probably insecure and wants to be with someone who he doesn't fear will hurt him.

Another chasing scenario is when you're dating a couple of guys fairly frequently—once or twice a week—and you want a commitment from one of them. No matter how many people you date at a time, there's always one who captures your attention the most. If you're following my advice, you let the men you date know up front that you aren't exclusive and that you date other men. This is step one in getting him to make his move. The more attached he becomes, the more he won't be able to stand the thought of you with another man. Keep things light and fun—never discuss getting serious. Guys are used to women pushing for this and will be surprised by the fact that you aren't. I know a lot of men who quit seeing a woman the minute she starts to get serious. Honestly, that just means he wasn't that into her to begin with. Don't talk about other men in front of the guy you're dating. That's rude and he will clearly see through you—he'll know you're trying to make him jealous. Keep him in suspense about the other men in your life. He'll wonder how he measures up and try harder to impress you.

Your tactics are working and the man you desire asks for a commitment—he wants to date exclusively. You know how I feel about this, but make your decision based on your own opinion. If you're crazy about him and no longer want to keep your options open, go for it. Ask yourself a few important questions. Can I see myself spending the rest of my life with this man? Do I have the desire to be with another man? Am I satisfied with the lifestyle I will have in this relationship? Do I want to change something about him, or do I love him the way he is? If he meets all of these needs, I don't see the problem with dating him exclusively. If there's something missing, keep dating him—just don't commit.

Many forms of manipulation come into play when pursuing another person. I have a tendency to mirror the man I'm with. This comes naturally from my sales background and actually works like a charm. Men tell me all the time that they think I'm their female version. Every guy likes himself, and enjoys being around someone who makes him comfortable with who he is. I'm not suggesting that you agree with everything he says, like the same music he does, or show interest in the same things he enjoys. That's boring. Try to mirror his way of being. If he's worldly and polished, show him that side of you. If he's casual and easygoing, be the same. A high-maintenance woman has all these traits and can demonstrate the appropriate personality for the occasion. There are many sides to me, which is why I enjoy dating different types of men. Some days I want to wear designer clothes and travel in style; on others I want to throw on a pair of jeans and go to a sports bar. To pull the mirroring tactic off, you must hone your skills. If you try to be something you're not, it will show.

We've touched on getting what you want, which is fairly simple when you do the right things. The hard part is wanting what you have. You found your dream guy, got swept off your feet, and married him—now what? It's inevitable for complacency and boredom to set in. The chase is over, the challenge is gone, and, before you know it, you're restless. Your never-ending job is to keep the spark alive. A couple has to work diligently at making each other feel appreciated and loved. Too often we take the person closest to us for granted and, as a result, he slowly slips away. As a woman, a wife, it is up to you to keep your man attracted to you. Keep your body fit, your appearance alluring, and your personality endearing. Nobody likes a nag and, I guarantee you, a man doesn't want you to try to change him. You knew what you were getting into when you married him—love him as he is.

In a relationship as well as a marriage there will be times when you start to think there is something better out there. Stop to analyze your personal situation and what is lacking. Try to look at the positives and why you fell in love with this person in the first place. Give yourself an attitude adjustment, plan a romantic evening, and work at rekindling your love affair. I've been single and longed for a relationship, married and desperate for freedom. The grass isn't always greener once you get there. When I truly looked at what was troubling me, I realized *I* was the problem. I didn't know what I wanted. I gave myself permission to take time off from feeling like I had to live up to other people's expectations and decided to "try on" all walks of life. I now live my life as I see fit, enjoying everything life has to offer and making no apologies for it. Once I "find myself" I will be ready to commit to the right man for the right reasons, but, until then, I'm going to enjoy the journey.

How To Win the Heart of a High-Maintenance Woman

As promised, gentlemen—this chapter is for you. I am going to let you in on a little secret. A drop-dead gorgeous, intelligent woman is waiting for you. All you have to do is learn what it takes to win her heart.

First, polish your image and attitude. Hire an image consultant or enlist one of your female friends to assist you. A high-maintenance woman wants her man to look great when she is by his side, so don't let her down. Let's address your wardrobe. If your jeans are Levis and your shoes are loafers, we have a lot of work to do. Don't lose hope—with a few simple purchases you'll be on your way. No matter what your age or profession, you can and should include a few trendy pieces in your ensemble. A pair of designer jeans and a Prada button-down look great on just about anyone. Find a nice balance between conservative and trendy. Opt for a classic look, with Gucci being one of the best choices. Once you have a woman in your life, take her shopping with you and let her choose some pieces for you to wear that she especially likes. This is usually one of the first things I do with the new man in my life. I work with a skilled sales associate to fill multiple dressing rooms with clothes I'd like to see my guy in. He then tries everything on, modeling it for me while I decide what looks best. He gets doted on, leaves with a new look, and I have arm candy, my stylish man.

Every man looks great in a well-tailored suit, so make sure you have at least one black, one blue, and one pinstripe suit in the closet.

Photography: Kelly Blackmon
Hair: Sevin
Makeup: Olivia Johnson

You also need a tuxedo that fits. The look I love the most on a man is a black Paul Smith suit with a crisp white shirt unbuttoned just enough to reveal a little chest hair. A pair of polished Gucci shoes and a matching belt with a silver buckle finish it all off. Dab on a little Dolce & Gabbana cologne and you'll be a force to be reckoned with.

Attention to detail is a must when putting yourself together. Your hair and nails need to be groomed, your breath fresh. If you look good, you will feel good. Confidence is a must when dealing with this level of woman—just don't mistake arrogance for confidence.

You look and feel great—now get out there and meet the woman of your dreams. It's a good idea to know what it is you want in a woman before you try to find her. That way, you can easily weed out the ones who don't meet your needs. The worst thing you can do is get involved with a woman not of your caliber just to fill time and keep you company while you search for the person who truly does it for you. When you do finally find her, you'll be forced to break someone's heart. Stand on your own, freeing yourself of any commitment or obligation until you find your high-maintenance woman. She will not date a man who is married or has a girlfriend—no exceptions.

Free to roam and eager to meet your match, you face an exciting adventure. Enjoy getting to know many different types of women—this will help you understand what you truly want. When you meet the woman you wish to spend the rest of your life with, hold on and never let her go. Sweep her off her feet and make her your wife. You will live the life of a king from that day forward. Every high-maintenance woman knows how to spoil her man and, believe me, she'll spoil you if you let her.

Let's not get ahead of ourselves. First, you have to win her over—make her choose you above all others. This will be a challenge with much competition. If your ego is fragile, you may not want to play in this arena, for you stand a good chance at getting hurt. You may set your eyes on a beauty queen whom someone else wins. Don't lose hope—you always have an opportunity to win her back, if you're willing to put forth the effort.

A high-maintenance woman wants to be pursued, enjoying how it makes her feel, so give her the pleasure of the chase. Too many men walk away from a challenge, opting for the easy way out. They usually regret it in the end. Have you ever lost the love of your life to another man? Did you allow it to happen?

Here are a few pointers on how to behave with an elite woman. Always open her door for her, even when she's getting out of the car. Walk on the side of the curb closest to the road, protecting her from danger—this tactic goes very far because it's so unexpected. Make sure she understands why you are doing this so it doesn't go unnoticed. Stand when she gets up from the dinner table and again when she returns and pull out her chair.

When you invite a woman out to dinner, be sure to make reservations at a restaurant of her liking. Give her a few options, but be decisive if she is not. On a first date, it's smart to take her to a place where you're well known and catered to. I will never forget having dinner with a man and observing how the entire staff came over one by one to say hello and attend to his needs. They knew how he wanted his food prepared and that he likes his Amstel poured in a cold glass, a little at a time. I was intrigued more than anything because I'd never seen such doting on a man before. I admit I was impressed and agreed to see him again partly as a result of this display.

Learn the art of palm greasing and you will go far. People go out of their way for you when they know cash is the reward. I learned from a man I was dating just how much money can buy. He put cash in everyone's hand, ensuring we'd be catered to wherever we went. I've gone back to a place without him and was remembered because of his generosity.

Ask your date what she would like to eat and order for her. If she has a problem with that, she is not a high-maintenance woman and you should move on (after dinner of course). Be sure to pay close attention to what she likes and dislikes, what she drinks, and whether she eats dessert or not. These details will impress her on future dates when you order still water instead of sparkling, knowing she prefers it, or ask the chef to prepare her favorite, chocolate soufflé, a dessert that requires additional time.

A woman wants to feel that you're listening to her, interested in her character—not just her body. The worst thing you can do is give the impression that you're going through the obligatory motions of dinner and conversation just to get her into bed. If the only time you see her is for a quick dinner and then off to your place, she will soon conclude that you are interested in only one thing, sex. Make a point of planning a fun date or trip with her, showing her she's worth the effort. If not, she'll eventually move on to someone else while leaving you in the dust.

Dating is supposed to be fun and exciting, with the man in control, guiding the path of the relationship. Decide what you want from a woman and tell her. If you simply want a playmate to have fun with, let her know and drop your guard. Remember, not every woman wants to marry you and take your money, so don't let your paranoia stand between you and a great woman. If she's looking for a serious relationship or marriage, she'll tell you and either move on or play by your rules for a while. Either way, you were up-front and therefore free from guilt and obligation.

Now it's time to throw out all the women's lib garbage you've been force fed lately and open your mind up to good old chivalry. If a woman catches your eye, pursue her. Ignore your fear of rejection—a confidant man willing to approach a beautiful woman stands a far better chance at getting a date with her than the guy sitting at the bar afraid of the word no. He may get shot down a few times, but eventually he'll succeed. A woman does not want to have to pursue you and, more often than not, won't. It goes against her belief that a woman is the prey, not the hunter. So many guys tell me, "I don't hit on women." Great—but how do you meet them then? I've talked to a lot of guys I normally might not have simply because they had the guts to approach me.

Roles are very important in a relationship both casual and serious. I like a man to be a man in every way and me to be feminine. I love a strong man who takes care of me, not necessarily financially. I mean seeing to my needs and giving me direction. I like him to be the boss and am happy to follow his wishes as long as he shows me respect and consideration. In a marriage, I want my husband to be the head of the household, leading us in a positive direction. I will let him guide me and admire him for his strength. Be a man that deserves as well as commands respect and you will have it.

Little gestures go a long way. I went on a date with someone and within days received a beautiful bouquet of roses. On my way down to the concierge to pick them up, I kept racking my brain to figure out whom they were from. Maybe from the man I just quit dating who was trying to win me back or possibly from a guy I date on occasion, but haven't seen lately because of his travel schedule. No, they were from the new man in my life. He just went from the bottom of the roster to the top with one small gesture. I called to thank him and he said something that made a lot of sense to me. "Just when you think no one is thinking about you, you get a surprise to let you know they are." This means a lot to a woman. She wants to feel that she is on your mind when you're apart. All it takes is a phone call to a florist and a credit card—you go from zero to hero. My guy actually went to the florist in person, selecting each rose by hand. I could tell the difference—big points for him.

I'm going to let you in on a little secret; women like sex. Most women don't want to sleep around, preferring to have one sexual partner, but that doesn't mean they want to commit and marry you right away. We like the intimacy and safety of just one sexual partner, but the freedom to date other men. Come on, guys, work with us on this. If a woman is dating four different men and chooses to sleep with one of them, she wants to know this is going to be her sex buddy for more than one night. Most single women want sex every day, so don't step up to the plate if you can't swing the bat.

Men are happy to add names to their roster, but women are just the opposite. We don't go around bragging about how many men we've been with; in fact, we often lie about it. Let a woman know up front what your intentions are—that way she can decide whether to add you to her list. If you tell her this is a one-time deal, she may turn you down (then again she may not), but at least give her the option. It'll save you a lot of drama and keep your reputation intact. Women talk, and before you know it you won't be able to get a date.

Find out whether she's a shoe girl or massage fan, or whatever, and spoil her. Send her a bouquet of designer shoes or a masseuse to her house. She will be impressed by your creativity and you'll advance to the top of her list. Don't forget that those shoes will be worn to bed with you, making for a memorable night. Think outside the box when trying to sweep a woman off her feet. If you can't come up with anything great, ask a friend what works for him or question a female friend about what impressed her the most. With a little extra effort, you can have your pick of any woman you want.

Nice guys finish last. Do you believe that? As much as I hate to admit it, there is some truth to that statement. Women like a bad boy; they often make the sensitive man their friend and the bad boy their lover. There is something irresistible about a confident man who knows what he wants—and gets it. She wants to be dominated in bed, picked up and tossed on the bed, arms held down, and ravished. Pull her hair a little. Don't hurt her, but let her feel your strength.

I went out with one guy with the intention of only giving him that one date, but he changed my mind with one small move. We were standing by the bar when he took my arms and held them behind my back, pressing me against the bar and him. Let's just say he got my attention and scored another date. I went out with him a couple times, but ruled him out. However, I will always wonder what he would have been like in bed. If a guy pulls my hair slightly when he kisses me, it's a glimpse into how he'll be in bed. Take my word for it—get your foreplay down and you'll have a lot of power over a woman. The trick is to mix tender with aggressive. Keep her guessing and, whatever you do, don't be lazy or predictable. She will quickly lose interest and move on.

Your looks and attitude are important; just don't lose sight of your profession. A high-maintenance woman wants a successful man whom she can respect and look up to. You don't have to be a millionaire, but you do need the ability to show her a good time, so stay focused and earn those dollars. It's hard to impress a woman when she's footing the bill—that puts her in the driver's seat and changes the dynamics of the relationship.

Never let her pay the tab, no matter how much she offers. You will go down a notch in her eyes if you do so, I assure you. It's not about the money. Your investment in her time is the issue. Show her that nothing could stand in the way of spending time with her, especially money. If you're taking turns paying, she is pursuing you as much as you are pursuing her. Yuck. Another rule of etiquette that should be followed is that the one inviting should offer to pay. If I called a guy up and asked him to dinner, I should offer to pay. That would never happen because I don't pursue men, but, if I did, I would expect to foot the bill. Same for you. If you ask a woman out, plan the date and pick up the tab. End of story!

You need to stand out from other men. Find your strongest quality and use it. A woman is attracted to a man for various reasons—fame and fortune as well as good looks are the obvious ones, but don't discount your chances if you have none of the above. I was sitting by the pool at the Hotel Bel Air on a date when I saw the oddest couple. The man weighed at least 300 pounds and was wearing skin-hugging spandex swim trunks. The woman by his side looked to be Russian and was beautiful. My first opinion was that she was a prostitute and he was rich. As the day passed, I watched them intently and realized they were very much in love. I could tell by her body language and attitude toward him. Sometimes it's possible for a woman to fall for a man despite his looks and lack of wealth, but because of his charm and the way he treats her.

Romance is the way to go. Send flowers, write love letters, order champagne. It's easy, guys—just use your imagination. Knock her socks off! I am extremely hard to impress, but let me say that, when someone does impress me, I am smitten. Show her you're interested, but don't be overbearing. Give her room to miss you and think about you. Call often, but not too much. A woman wants to hear from you every day and will feel rejected if you don't call. Be careful not to let her take you for granted, though. She needs to put forth effort to win you as well. Don't keep tabs—simply do everything you can and she will follow suit.

Become a high-maintenance man and you will soon win the heart of a high-maintenance woman. You will make an amazing couple—a force to be reckoned with. Together, you will have everything you ever dreamed of—and more. What are you waiting for?

Suggested Reading

$\mathcal{H}$ere is a list of some books that I have read over the years in my quest to become a high-maintenance woman. Chose ones that you can relate to, as well as some that are out of your comfort zone. It is important to become well rounded; therefore you need to study many different topics—etiquette, sexuality, self-help, business, travel, and current events.

Etiquette
Peggy Post: *Emily Post Etiquette*
Nancy Tuckerman and Nancy Dunnan: *The Amy Vanderbilt Complete Book of Etiquette*

Sexuality
Lonnie Barbach, Ph.D.: *Seductions/Tales of Erotic Persuasion*
The Editors of *Penthouse* Magazine: *Penthouse Uncensored*
Laura Corn: *101 Nights of Great Sex*
Laura Corn: *52 Invitations to Great Sex*
Dr. Alex Comfort: *The Joy of Sex*
William Cane: *The Art of Kissing*
Anne Hooper: *Great Sex Games*
Claudia Varrin: *Erotic Surrender/The Sensual Joys of Female Submission*

Siobhan Kelly: *The Ann Summers Guide to Wild Sex and Loving*
Robert Greene: *The Art of the Seduction*

Self-Help
Greg Behrendt and Liz Tuccillo: *He's Just Not That into You*
Leil Lowndes: *How To Make Anyone Fall in Love with You*
Tracey Cox: *Superdate/How to Be One, How to Get One*
Stephen R. Covey: *The 7 Habits of Highly Effective People*
Myreah Moore and Jodie Gould: *Date Like a Man*
John Gray, Ph.D.: *Men Are From Mars, Women Are From Venus*
John Gray, Ph.D.: *Mars and Venus on a Date*
John Gray, Ph.D.: *Mars and Venus in the Bedroom*
John Gray, Ph.D.: *Mars and Venus in Love*

Business
Robert Kiyosaki: *Rich Dad Poor Dad*
Russ Whitney: *Millionaire Real Estate Mentor*
Terri Morrison, Wayne A. Conway, and George A. Borden: *Kiss, Bow,*
   or Shake Hands: How To Do Business in Sixty Countries
John Tuccillo, Ph.D.: *The Eight New Rules of Real Estate*
Dr. Criswell Freeman: *The Salesman's Book of Wisdom*

Travel
Herbert Ypma: *Hip Hotels Beach*
Herbert Ypma: *Hip Hotels City*
Herbert Ypma: *Hip Hotels Escape*
Herbert Ypma: *Hip Hotels France*
Herbert Ypma: *Hip Hotels Italy*
Herbert Ypma: *Hip Hotels Ski*
Herbert Ypma: *Hip Hotels USA*

Current Topics
Rowman & Littlefield: *Middle East Illusions*
Benjamin R. Barber: *Jihad Versus McWorld*
Cohn-Sherbok & El-Alami: *The Palestine—Israeli Conflict*